Prison 101:
A Tutorial for
the Uninitiated

Paul L. Martin, M.Sc.

PRISON 101: A TUTORIAL FOR THE UNINITIATED

Printed in the United States of America

ISBN: 9781519693754

Dedication

THIS BOOK IS dedicated to those who are no longer with us:

Greg Day, a true friend and brother, of New Martinsville (Wetzel County), West Virginia.

Clyde Meadows, my sister-in-law Mary Jones' brother and friend of Shenandoah County, Virginia.

When Carolyn L. Barkley, who began the initial transcription of this book, first learned of her terminal illness, she actually apologized to me in the case that it delayed my book! She was a consummate professional and a thoughtful, selfless soul of Roseland, Virginia.

All three are greatly loved and missed by many, myself included.

Acknowledgements

I TAKE THIS opportunity to thank all those who have positively impacted my life and supported me in all my endeavors, including the writing of this book: Dr. Ann Paterson; Dr. Alan Jenks; Dr. Robert White; Dr. Ted Koebel; Dr. William Wallace; James and Dorcas Good; Ruth Horst; George and Mary Jones; Bob and Jan Gardner-Harris; John T. Hazel; Carolyn Barkley; Ted Malone; Andrew Houff; J.M. Snyder; Chaplain Tommy Armstrong; Brenda McCaman; the Day family; and so many others to whom I owe a debt of gratitude. Thank you.

Table of Contents

Introduction

LIFE INSIDE PRISON is like traveling to a foreign land where one does not know the language, the culture, and hasn't a clue how to navigate its environs. Many myths surround prison life. Hollywood has propagated the mythology of prisons as have politicians. While the genesis of such myths is based on fact, they have been embellished beyond recognition. Books have been written by offenders offering a personal view of their experiences. One journalist obtained a job in a New York State prison and wrote of his experiences. Since these accounts are based on personal experiences, they cannot help but be biased. While I have endeavored to present a fair and balanced account in this work, it too has a bias. It is my hope that with that knowledge in mind, the reader may better discern the truth.

Someone once said that the hardest part of "doing time" is dealing with the people with whom one must interact, staff and offenders alike. It is nearly impossible to navigate prison life successfully without some understanding of the people one encounters there. Offenders do not come into prison as newborns. We all come into this environment with life experiences which have shaped our respective worldviews. Once incarcerated, there are a variety of issues one must confront and address.

One must develop the ability to discern the proper path for life while imprisoned to work toward meeting achievable goals post-imprisonment. Institutions offer a variety of programs (treatment, educational, religious), but unfortunately the quality of instruction or facilitation may be poor due to staff incompetence. Even so, one can glean useful information and learn positive lessons. One can learn a lot even from the most negative of experiences. You can easily become discouraged while incarcerated, but must fight off such emotions. You can easily despair over life post-prison, for civil government and society-at-large are often failures when it comes to the repatriation of their citizens. Records show that they have been utter failures in reintegrating former offenders into their respective communities. The focus has, until recently, solely been on punishment. Offenders exit confinement to reenter a world where they are discriminated against openly and are continually made to feel as outcasts. Each negative experience reinforces the label, and eventually offenders will buy into it and act accordingly. Their actions are detrimental not only to themselves and their families, but also to their respective communities, taxpaying citizens, and civil society at large.

This much I know for sure however; open doors spring up from the most unlikely places and assistance comes from the most unlikely people. However, the common denominator is that one must do his or her part to help oneself, preparing for the day a door of opportunity will be opened and/or someone will come to one's aid. I've experienced this phenomenon too many times to count.

Two seemingly contradictory sources opened my eyes to unexpected opportunity. The first source was the United States Marine Corps. Even though I screwed up there, I learned that "SEMPER FIDELIS" (Always Faithful) is much more than a motto. Over the years of my incarceration my fellow Marines and former Marines have come to my aid numerous times.

The second source is my Catholic faith which has enabled me to survive the most negative of experiences. It taught me to trust God and learn to be dependent on Him alone. I have lived a blessed life in spite of those negative experiences, for my Creator has always loved me and never abandoned me. He has been with me when I was rebellious, disobedient, prideful, or angry, and the most wonderful thing is that He knows the worst about me and loves me nonetheless. Others may abandon or betray me but He never will. I may be lonely at times, but I am never alone for He is with me in the best of times and the worst of times. I pray that all of my readers may experience His love and acceptance as well.

Chapter 1
From Childhood to Manhood

I WAS BORN a bastard. Some would say that I've lived up to this label since my birth! My father, a Native American, was not married to my mother, a Caucasian. Back then, Native Americans were strongly discriminated against, and most attempted to hide their identity. Due to the actions of Walter Plecker, Director of Vital Statistics for the Commonwealth of Virginia at that time, Native Americans could not list their race accurately on their birth records, nor any Native American names. It was not until 1997 that this law was changed, thanks to the lobbying efforts of Ms. Diane Shields of the Monocan Nation and State Senator Thomas Norment. I first had to correct my father's birth record and then mine; I changed my own name from "Lee" to "Littletree."

When I was growing up there was much conflict in my family. My aunt and uncle once called the law on my parents because "cohabitation" had been illegal at the time. I remember my mom, my dad, and I walking to a church in Monroe, Virginia, where we met the pastor and he married my parents. I was just five or six years old at the time. Then we rode with my aunt and uncle to Amherst Circuit Court for the hearing on the cohabitation charge. Dad showed the judge the marriage license, and the charge was dropped. There were numerous other issues involving my dad's family while we lived in Monroe. Everyone except my mother drank a lot. My step-grandfather beat my paternal grandmother. There was always a lot of conflict, even a shooting once.

Native Americans and alcohol do not mix very well. My people used to make moonshine. One Saturday a bunch of us were in my grandmother's house sitting in a semi-circle, playing guitars and drinking. I was on the floor between my father's legs. Bill Pugh, a family friend and Monocan Indian, told my grandmother he thought the world of her and would do anything for her—all she had to do was ask. As calmly as you please, she replied, "Why don't you shoot one of those damned Ashleys?" Bill, just as calmly, pulled out a pistol and shot one of my adult cousins; my grandmother's own grandson, her daughter's son.

One would think that my father would have gotten me out of there, but he did not. Uncle Bob, my (now shot) cousin's father, grabbed me up, carried me across the dirt road to his place, put me in a closet, and told me not to come out until he came back for me. I was on my knees looking under the door when I soon heard someone. Then I saw blood dripping on the floor and knew it was my cousin. He walked off, and it got very quiet again. Eventually curiosity overcame me, so I came out of the closet and walked to the window facing the road. There I saw one of the strangest sights of my life. Bill Pugh was on the dirt road to my right, and my uncle and cousins were on the dirt road to my left. Bill was shooting at them with a pistol, but was so drunk he couldn't hit anything. They were all throwing rocks at Bill. But it was clear that no one wanted any harm to come to Bill; there were plenty of weapons available should anyone have wanted to hurt him. Eventually, the sheriff came. My memory of what happened next was Bill spending the weekend in jail, with no charges having been filed. And the next weekend there he was, back at grandma's house drinking again!

At one point we were in a bad wreck when a speeding car hit us from behind while we were turning off the main road. A man named

Coy Pugh was with me and my parents at the time. The car flipped over several times. I was sitting on my mother's lap and was thrown out the windshield and onto the pavement. The car actually flipped over me. When the rescue squad arrived, Mom was leaning against the car with her arms around me as I stood in front of her. I was covered in blood, but it wasn't mine. It was my mother's. She had sustained a severe head injury.

Since Dad could not read or write, he had thought the Division of Motor Vehicles (DMV) uninsured motorist fee was insurance. The wreck had not been his fault, but the drunken woman who had hit us was politically connected within the county social network, and my dad was faulted for the wreck and lost his driver's license. Prior to that, he had driven a dump truck for E.G. Sprouse in Madison Heights, but he now had to get a job at Rockydale Stone Quarry in Campbell County. We then moved to Fairview Heights in Lynchburg. Dad caught a ride to and from work with a guy he knew who also worked at the rock quarry.

Mom's head injury really changed her. She had been mentally ill beforehand, but afterwards she was angry a lot more often and even had begun to have seizures. She'd had three sons from a previous marriage but did not raise them. My father had two daughters and a son of his own from a previous marriage, but he did not raise his children, either. I was the only child my two parents had ever raised. Dad's kids resented me for this, but they shouldn't have, for my parents truly did not do me any favors in raising me as they did. I never felt accepted by my father's children, however my mother's sons all accepted me.

One Christmas while we were in the Shenandoah Valley visiting my brothers Charlie and George, my siblings called me in to the dining room to talk. I had thought I was in trouble at the time, but they told me that they loved me—that to them I was not their half-brother, but their brother! I couldn't believe it! Unfortunately, I got to see them only once or twice a year.

For all my formative years, my mother would go on crying binges and beat me severely, until she was completely spent - too tired to continue. I had feared her so much that I even let other children beat me with their fists without retaliating. My close childhood friend, Brian Travis, begged me to defend myself, but I had been too ashamed to tell him why I would not fight back. At one point, I actually believed my mother would kill me. I never told my dad because I believed that he would only tell Mom, and then I'd really get hurt. The beatings other kids gave me paled in comparison to what Mom would do.

I even got beaten for telling the truth. Prior to the car accident, when I was four or five, my mother and I went to a man's house. I was given some milk and cookies and a small record player that used 45's (45 rpms). Mom told me to stay put, that she would be right back. They went in to this man's bedroom for quite a while. That evening I was so excited about using the record player that as soon as Dad came home, I told him everything. My mother—in a rage— ran at me and started smacking me in the face while screaming that I was a liar and should not be telling lies! Imagine how confusing that was to a small child!

Another time after the car accident, while I was in elementary school, I had been so excited that my brother Johnny was coming home from prison. Mom told me that I did not even have to go to school that day. I told my friends that I would not be in school because my brother would be coming home. I was extremely happy because I had really looked up to my brother. One of my most treasured possessions had been a photo of my brother and me at the federal prison in which he had been housed in Petersburg, Virginia.

The other kids and teachers did not believe me about my mom allowing me to stay home and they even asked her. When this happened, she once again immediately began smacking me hard in the face, yelling at me to quit telling lies. I was humiliated! And after all this, my brother ended up coming home from prison the next day.

One day when I was about thirteen years old, my dad saw a guy beating me (in the face, as usual) while I just stood there taking it. While we were walking home, Dad asked me why I hadn't fought back. I just could not keep the secret any longer, so I told Dad all that Mom had done to me over the years. He actually looked angry, which scared me. I've witnessed him delivering a beating of his own to seven or eight guys at once without difficulty, so I definitely did not want him angry with me.

Dad told me not to worry about my mother, that he would take care of her. Then he told me to go across the street and fight the guy who had been hitting me. I immediately did as he said. The strange thing is that the guy who had been hitting me now cried out, asking me why I had hit him! I vowed that day that I would never let anyone put their hands on me ever again without my beating the daylights out of them! Thus marks the genesis of my rage.

I idolized my father for most of my life. I've seen him work even while suffering from pneumonia. I saw him fight and viewed him as a warrior. I glossed over the fact that he thought I was not his biological son due to my mother's promiscuity, that he resented me for it and viewed me as a burden. I also casually overlooked the fact that he had essentially ignored me for thirteen years. Over the course of all those years, I never heard a kind word from him. He would talk to me when he was drunk, but only then. Most of the time when he was drunk, he beat Mom, and we often had to escape and spend the night outdoors. He even tried cutting me with a blade once when I had pushed him off Mom while he had been beating on her. Fortunately he had been too drunk to catch me at the time! Once he flat out told me to get away from him, needlessly chastising me that I "couldn't stand up in a ten-acre field without falling down."

I cannot remember Dad ever having taught me anything. For all intents and purposes, he was absent for the first thirteen years of my life. For years I had hated my mother and idolized my father from a distance. But Dad and I eventually even became close.

Strangely enough and of all times, it was during an incident in which I was trying to shoot at another guy that I learned my father truly loved me. As it went, the guy had been in a crowd, and I fired my first shot with the shotgun. As everyone scattered, I reloaded. Out of nowhere my mother came and grabbed the end of the shotgun, yelling at me, but I never heard a word she had said. I pulled the barrel out of her grip, pointed it to the sky, and pulled the trigger so as to not shoot her by mistake. The moment I did this, I saw a sight that shocked me. My dad, the stoic and tough Native American that he was, had tears running down his face. All he kept saying was, "Son, please don't shoot him. Give me the gun, son; give me the gun." This shocked me so much that I calmly stopped and handed over the shotgun.

A short time after this, I was hanging out across the street in the parking lot of Warren's restaurant one day. We used to congregate there around the phone booths and the restaurant sign. On this occasion, a guy pulled up asking for directions. When I walked over to him, he pulled a pistol on me and told me to get in the car. Instead of doing as he asked, I knocked the pistol out of his hand, and it fell to the floorboard of the car. I then grabbed him and started beating on him relentlessly with my fists. Someone handed me a truck wrench, and I beat him with that, too. Fortunately, my mother came running across the street and got in between me and the guy. She yelled at him to get out of there before I killed him. He took off, and I got a friend to take me to the emergency room because I was so incensed that I wanted to finish what I had started and figured he would be there. But he was not.

I had mentioned before that my mother was mentally ill: Well, after all she put me through, she beat me severely yet one more time. I remember when it was over thinking it was odd that she had begun washing dishes like nothing had even happened. Afterward, I walked out of the room, got my shotgun, and loaded it. I'd had it pointed directly at the back of her head and was about to pull the trigger when a loud voice inside my head told me to stop. I quickly unloaded the weapon and returned it to its storage space. My mother never even knew how close she had come to dying. Thank God for that Voice! A few weeks later she attempted to beat me again, but I just pinned her arms down by her sides and told her that she would never put her hands on me again. And so she never did.

As you can see, I was raised in a very dysfunctional and violent family. I was slow to learn in school because my parents were illiterate. The only book in our home was a Bible, and no one could even read it until I learned to do so. Things were so rough I didn't even know what shampoo was! One day two girls I knew, Donna Brewer and Brenda Love, asked me why I did not wash my hair. I told them I washed it daily with soap. They actually had to explain to me how shampoo worked and how to use it! Mine was a family so poor that we thought folks on welfare were wealthy. "Section 8" apartments had been built recently on Florida Avenue, and the people there dressed nicely and had cars. They were doing a lot better than we were. However, I never knew I was poor until a girl who lived in those apartments asked me why I never changed clothes; I explained that I had two pairs and that Mom would hand wash one set each day. The girl told me she was sorry that I only had two pairs of school clothes. At the time, I did not even understand why she had felt sorry for me.

As a kid, I had a paper route and shined shoes in Frank Dodson's barber shop. When I turned fourteen, Warren Falwell (Jerry Falwell's uncle) let me wash dishes in his restaurant. I would work into the night then hang out in the parking lot with the others. Shirley Jones, an African-American waitress, would come outside and call for me—under the pretense that she needed help sweeping and mopping the floor—just to get me away from the crowd. Mrs. Fleishman, the cook, treated me like a grandson. These women loved me—even as my own family couldn't have cared less. As both Mrs. Fleishman and Ms. Jones were black, however, they were only allowed to cook the food and serve it but were not permitted to sit down in the restaurant to eat; no black folks could then. If they did want to buy food, they would have to come to the cash register to place their order, pay for it, and then leave with it. It never made any sense to me.

My next door neighbor, Mr. Gillespie, was a barrel-chested man with huge arms who used to tease me about getting some "stovepipes," as he referred to his own huge arms. He would stay up late at night until I came in, and as I passed by his place, he'd ask where I'd been. Meanwhile, my parents were sleeping soundly without a care in the world. Years later, I took great pleasure in showing Mr. Gillespie my own "stovepipes!"

I began to drink alcohol early in my childhood years. Most of my family was alcoholics, and our being of Native American heritage did not help. I also used drugs to deaden my pain. I was fearless, for I did not care whether I lived or died. It just did not matter to me. I've had people try to stab me, cut, and shoot at me. I've fought some and fired shots at others, myself. Although I am essentially a very shy and reserved person, I got into a wild crowd growing up and began to burglarize businesses and doctor's offices. I was among those who broke in Frank Dodson's brother Bert's pest control business. I truly regret this.

Of all of us who spent our youth in that part of Fairview Heights, only my true childhood friend Brian Travis went on to do well in life without getting into trouble first. He was a good person himself, but his sainted mother sacrificed much to send him to Jerry Falwell's Lynchburg Christian Academy, and she never let him become involved in all the craziness of the neighborhood. I often wonder what would have happened if I'd had the same opportunity.

Our gang eventually got arrested, and I began my experience with the juvenile justice system, where many staff members and offenders alike had my best interests at heart and tried getting me on the right path. However, I was so messed up mentally and emotionally due to my childhood traumas and substance abuse that these erstwhile efforts bore no immediate fruit.

There is one more trauma worth noting that for most of my life I've felt too ashamed to ever mention. When I was in elementary school a neighborhood teenager molested me. I felt shame down to my core. This single act attacked my masculinity—not to mention that as a teenager I had been extremely shy around girls my own age but this was not so with older women. At one point I actually became a male prostitute. It was business, not personal, though, and surprisingly, I wasn't shy at all. It was easy money for someone who grew up poor as I did. I thought I had hit the jackpot!

Eventually I was arrested for the burglaries I had committed. Initially I was placed on probation and sent to Opportunity House on Belvedere Street. Dan Roop, Gary Harper, Ms. Washington, and Jo Davidson at the probation department were especially kind to me. At the house Mrs. Stratton was the cook and essentially the house mother. She taught me table manners and always had good jokes to tell. I ate food there that I had never even seen before. Her son, Tom Stratton, encouraged me to have goals and taught me how to write them down. Mrs. Ferguson was like a favorite aunt to me, she even let me sip a little bit of Irish coffee! Joan Campbell did her best to help me overcome my issues. The director, Gibbs Arthur, taught me progressive muscle relaxation techniques, among other things. Mr. Arthur understood me a little better after he witnessed my uncle and cousins, who lived nearby, fighting. When the police came, they all turned on the police and attacked them, too. I was laughing about this, and Mr. Arthur asked me what was funny. I told him they were my relatives, and that they did this type of thing all the time. One would think the cops would have figured this out by now.

In another event, I overdosed on pills and was sent to Rubicon in Richmond, Virginia for treatment. I lasted only twenty some days there before I got kicked out. Judge Earl Wingo did not lock me up, though, so one of my brothers and I hitchhiked to Alexandria, Virginia. We lived on the street for a couple of weeks before finding jobs (me at Drug Fair on Duke Street, and my brother with Alexandria Diamond Cab). We rented a room together from Mrs. Furr on Duke Street in Alexandria.

One weekend, while my brother was away with one of his girlfriends, I decided to catch the bus home to see my parents. At the bus station on New York Avenue in D.C., I ran into my brother and his girlfriend. They asked me to stay around, but I told them I would be back Sunday night. Little did I know that this would not happen.

Not long after my arrival at my parents' place, Officer Johnson of the Lynchburg Police Department came and arrested me on a charge of theft of a tractor and trailer. I then spent several months in the local detention home where I'd been before. While I was there the staff treated me especially well. They even did so after I assaulted a college student who had been working there. I felt sick at the time, and this guy kept getting after me to participate in arts and crafts. I asked him to leave me alone and put my head down on the table. He started in on me again, and so I hit him—hard. He landed in the adjacent sink. Staff members scooped me up and put me in my cell for a week or two. By then I was feeling better. When I went to court the original charge was dropped, but I had attempted to attack the guy for lying about me and ended up assaulting several police officers afterward. For the assaults I was sent to reform school, Beaumont Learning Center, near Richmond.

I had positive experiences at Beaumont. I had an excellent bricklaying instructor who was a retired Seabee. My G.E.D. instructor was also a graduate student at Virginia Commonwealth University in Richmond. He would loan me his texts on African literature and encouraged my desire to learn.

From Beaumont I was sent to a halfway house on Second Street in Roanoke, Virginia. The female counselor helped me to find a job. Tony Leger, my counselor, helped me out tremendously with a lucky situation. My girlfriend, Nora Rutherford, had moved with her mother to Florida. Nora ran off, and her mother called Tony, telling him I had kidnapped her daughter. I happened to be working on a ranch in nearby Franklin County at the time. When I returned from work on this particular day, Tony called me in to the office and explained the situation to me. More importantly, he explained how upset Nora's mother was and that I should not take personally anything she had said over the phone. He then let me call Nora's mom and explain that I had nothing to do with Nora running off and that I would contact her should I hear from Nora. At first she gave me hell but soon calmed down and actually apologized for being upset with me. The cops caught Nora near her old home, and I never did see or hear from her again.

Upon my release from the halfway house, I was sent home and placed on five years' probation. I knew I'd never make it the way things had been going, so I talked my legal guardian, the director of the halfway house, into signing off for me to enlist in the Marine Corps. I had an overarching need to prove my masculinity due to my being molested in the past. In my mind, no one was more masculine than a Marine. Since I was only seventeen, I could not yet sit for the G.E.D. examination in Virginia, where one had to be eighteen. Since this was the case, Sgt. Charlie Isennock arranged for me to take the examination at the South Branch Vocational-Technical Center in Petersburg, West Virginia. He also helped me get approved for enlistment.

I enlisted through the delayed enlistment program, so I was allowed to go home for a few months. During that time, the recruiter in Lynchburg had to return to New Orleans due to his mother's illness. The "gunny," or gunnery sergeant, had me man the recruiting station for a couple of weeks. I made recruiting phone calls and handed out literature to enquirers. The gunny would come down each evening, and I set up appointments for people to see him. He promised me a promotion for doing the work, and I received it right out of boot camp. Also while there I read that I had a choice of where to go to boot camp, so I chose MCRD in San Diego.

Infantry and rifle training were conducted at Camp Pendleton. The day before my rifle qualification, I received a letter written on behalf of my father informing me that my parents were about to lose their mobile home. Before I got to boot camp, my father had almost died in a very bad truck accident. The pickup truck he had been riding home in from work collided with a disabled dump truck. Afterward, Dad went on disability and could not work. He was waiting for the funds from a lawsuit against the dump truck's owner and for his Social Security to "kick in."

I am a pretty good shot, however while on the firing range the next day I could not hit the broad side of a barn. One of the range instructors pulled me off the line and asked me what my problem was. I explained the situation with my father, and he escorted me to a captain's office where I also explained the situation to the Captain. He asked me how much money I needed and told me to write down the address where I wanted the funds sent. The Captain told me that the funds would go out that very morning! I couldn't thank him enough! He explained that the loan would be taken out of my pay every two weeks. The disturbing thing was that Dad's children lived nearby, as did numerous other family members of ours. None of them would assist him. One sister of mine used to charge him to go and pay his bills at places she had to go anyway—this shows the lack of love and loyalty.

I graduated from boot camp and was assigned to Infantry Training School at Camp Pendleton, where I graduated as 0341 mortar man. My original orders were to Okinawa, Japan, but while I was in line to get some shots at medical, an officer passed by, stopped, and came back asking me for my identification card. He then told me not to move; I thought I was in trouble. However, he'd had my orders changed on the spot to Marine Barracks, Pearl Harbor, Hawaii. One of my uncles had been in the Navy there in 1941 when the Japanese attacked. I was excited to be able to go there!

I flew out of Los Angeles airport (LAX) with Daniel K. Jones from Bristol, Virginia, and Ron Lewis who was from Illinois and Texas. We reported to the colonel and were told that we had liberty until 0600 the following day. We caught the bus into Honolulu. I pulled the cord (instructing the bus driver to stop) at a particular spot that later held some significance for me. We had stopped at Hotel Street, which was full of strip clubs, topless bars, and tattoo parlors.

I got a tattoo at the China Sea Tattoo Parlor just off Hotel Street behind Tammy's, another topless bar. I dated girls from those clubs. After my Dad's lawsuit was settled, he and Mom came over and spent a week on base at a beach rental and a second week in Honolulu in a hotel. I showed them the sights and took Dad to one of the clubs where I got one of the girls to flirt with him. Dad kept looking around, and I asked him what was wrong. He asked me if we could get raided by the police! I laughed and told him it was all legal, not to worry. Then I remembered that Dad had lived through the Prohibition era.

D.K. Jones, Ron Lewis, and I were posted to Marine Barracks, Naval Air Station, Barber's Point. In World War II it was called Ewa Field because it sits adjacent to Ewa Beach on the ocean, just down the mountain from Makakilo. The leadership of my posting gave those enlisted there on-the-job training, for back then there was no school for our job as there is now. Now, the Corps has Security Forces Battalion, a training facility located at Little Creek,

Virginia, if I remember correctly. We provided base perimeter security and nuclear weapons security and were assigned body guard detail plus ceremonial duties. I received a Department of Defense (DOD) security clearance, a nuclear weapon security clearance, and continual training in weapons.

At one point, President Jimmy Carter, Secretary of Defense Harold Brown, and several other upper-level government figures met on our base for talks on Korea. Our unit provided perimeter security for the President, and we had to wave the officials in once they arrived at the base.

When Angie Dickenson and Dennis Weaver filmed the movie *Pearl*, I was manning the main gate and waved them in. I had a very interesting conversation with one of the crew about this film and an earlier one, *Tora, Tora, Tora*. We also had to participate in sunset parades at Pearl Harbor, retirement ceremonies, and ceremonies for foreign dignitaries.

I held a part-time job off base working for a wealthy guy who had many famous friends. One of his lesser known enterprises was a very discrete escort service. Old habits die hard.

I was still buck wild and drank and smoked a lot. The leadership of my unit attempted to get me straight. I had many issues. I got into many fights. Once I fought some Black Marines because they did not like the fact that I was friends with another black Marine, and we would hang out together. I expected that crap from the white guys, but not the black guys. The First Sergeant accused me of racism! Thus began the beginning of the end for me at that unit. However, Gunny Sgt. Newman tried to encourage me to do better. I had been getting into fights a lot, so he put in for me to compete for Marine of the Month for Marine Barracks Hawaii. Our unit had not won this distinction for years. At first I thought he was joking, but he was not. He actually believed in me, and that meant a lot to me. The sergeant major headed up a board before which candidates from each unit had to appear. They had thoroughly examined our service record books prior to our interviews. In the end it came down to me and one other Marine.

If memory serves me correctly, I was only asked one question:

"Who is the best Marine in your unit?" Of course, my response to this was a question, as well: "Do you mean—besides me?" This pretty much sealed the deal. As the winner, I received a free weekend (off-duty) at the Holiday Inn at Honolulu International Airport. I had my picture taken with two wahinis (native women) dressed in traditional Hawaiian clothing. And we were all wearing leis. I was also supposed to receive an automatic promotion, but due to my past issues, the Colonel delayed it. I was very immature at the time, and while this promotional delay was very reasonable, it truly angered me.

Not long afterward I left Hawaii with three other disgruntled Marines. We flew out of Honolulu on the night of Friday the thirteenth. Halfway to Seattle, we went through a very violent storm with lightning and thunder. We all were very happy when the plane landed.

We caught a bus going south through Portland, Oregon, with a layover in Sacramento. During that ride I met an older Inuit fellow from Kodiak, Alaska. He had many jokes and made that portion of the ride very enjoyable. During the layover in Sacramento, we visited a tattoo parlor. The guy there saw the tattoo that I had gotten in Hawaii and actually was able to name the person who did it! He knew they guy's work that well. We caught another bus and traveled through Reno, Nevada, and Salt Lake City, Utah, and on to Denver, Colorado. We spent some time in the Denver area, then bought an old 1960 Dodge truck with no radio and a third gear missing. We drove straight through to my brother's apartment in Alexandria, Virginia. As we entered the parking lot, the truck engine died, and we drifted into a parking space.

I had hooked up with one of my brother's ex-girlfriends, who was ten years older than me. She started talking about marriage, but I was not interested. That is, not until my brother angrily told me not to even consider marrying her but wouldn't say why. He made me so angry that we were married at once by a magistrate at the Alexandria Courthouse. I was in jeans, a surfing shirt, and beach sandals; I was also still absent without leave from the Marine Corps. At one point I lived next door to an army brigadier general and had a friend who was a navy captain stationed at the Pentagon, not to mention secret service agents. I did not hide at all and worked in construction under my own name and Social Security number.

My brother convinced me to get my hacker's license so that I could drive his cab part time. I took the exam, but when I went to pick up the license, I was held for the Navy Shore Patrol who came and took me to the Washington Navy Yard near my mother-in-law's place in Southeast D.C. They made me dry shave my beard, took my mug shot, and finger printed me. Then they transported me to the brig at Quantico Marine Base, where I spent the weekend. On Monday I was assigned to the Provost Marshal's office (Casual Section) and could go home each night and all weekends.

I found out that my wife cheated on me with her ex-husband the weekend I was in the brig. I also later learned that she was not divorced when she and I were married. Then I had an affair with a woman whom I truly loved. She was three years younger than me. It turns out that we had a son I did not know about. He was adopted by a good family. I never knew he was my son until years later after I had met him in one of the prisons I was in before I was transferred away. I truly regret never being a part of his life.

I eventually decided to sign paperwork for a General Discharge from the Marine Corps under other than Honorable Conditions, for I had been AWOL for just over 180 days. I have regretted this decision ever since. It was one of the poorest decisions I've made in life.

Chapter 2
Experiencing Prison, Probation, and Parole

THE MARINE CORPS taught me many valuable lessons. It taught me that I could survive anything and could overcome any adversity. This knowledge came in handy a little over a year after I my discharge from the Corps. Prior to my imprisonment in Florida, I was hired in Northern Virginia for a carpentry job in St. Augustine Shores, just south of St. Augustine, Florida. I lived there on Alcala Drive. My backyard was on the Intracoastal Waterway, and I could see St. Augustine Beach and the Atlantic Ocean from my backyard. Alligators would come out of the water and snort at their images in the sliding glass doors in the back of the house.

I was still drinking at the time and wrote several bad checks in St. Augustine, Palatka, and Jacksonville. I was initially arrested in Palatka but jumped bail and returned to Virginia. Eventually I ended up at one of my sister's apartments. Her husband reported me to the police, and the SWAT team came and arrested me. I knew they were coming, as I saw one of the snipers on a rooftop across the side street in advance. I spent a few months in jail and then was flown to Brunswick, Georgia, where I spent the night in jail and flew into St. Augustine the next day. I was handcuffed and shackled the whole way.

I was then taken to St. John's County Jail. I was treated extremely well there by all those concerned. I had interesting cell partners. One was a New York butcher who had cut up his wife and packaged and labeled her body parts. Another, an Italian-American barber from St. Louis, had cut up a number of women. I would get him to cut my hair and others thought I was crazy for doing so. I told them I wasn't in any danger, for I was not a woman and had not done anything to make him mad at me!

One group of guys escaped several times, two of them brothers from Northern Virginia. The first time they escaped the two came by my cell and asked if I wanted to go. I declined but thanked them for thinking of me. After getting away, they'd go out and rob jewelry stores and then party until they got busted.

About the third or fourth time they attempted to escape, it was a set up. The police started shooting, and I heard bullets ricocheting. As crazy as it sounds, I pulled the mattress off my bunk, climbed under the bunk, and pulled the mattress in behind me! I guess I thought it would keep me from being shot! I never saw either of those guys again. Later on I was at Baker Correctional Institute with one of the escapees, John Smith. He is the only one I ever did see again.

Hamilton Upschurch, Jr., represented me in St. Augustine. I received two two-year sentences to be served concurrently. I was transferred to Duval County Jail in Jacksonville, a high rise building on the riverfront. In Jacksonville I was given a court appointed attorney who was great. He wanted to take my charges to trial. I told him I already had a prison sentence, to just get me something to run concurrently with it. He did not like this, but he did it anyway. I was taken to the courtroom where Judge Sao had just given a guy the death penalty! I thought I was so screwed! However, he recessed court for fifteen minutes and told the bailiff to take me out of the courtroom. Upon my return there was a different judge. I cannot fully remember his name but I saw him years later on the Florida Supreme Court when they ruled on *Bush v. Gore*. This judge gave me a one year concurrent sentence plus five years of probation. Strangely enough, the probation started right then. Later, I was in prison and on probation at the same time.

I was transported by the Grey Goose (bus) to Lake Butler Reception Center. As I was taken to K-Wing, I saw a dead prisoner hanging on the perimeter fence. There were some notorious guards there with memorable nicknames like "K-Wing Slim," "Nigga Charlie," and "Breezeway Red," a former Raiford lifer who saved a guard's life. I never thought of Florida as the Deep South, but one incident opened my eyes to this fact.

The black guy in the cell next to me in K-Wing was raising hell about something one day. An old white guard came to his cell and told him to come to the bars so he could show him something. The guard pulled out his wallet and showed him a card, something like a membership card. He then told the prisoner that it would be in his best interest to settle down and shut up. The prisoner immediately did so. Later on I asked the guy what was on the guard's card. He told me it was a KKK membership card!

I was transferred to Baker Correctional Institute in Olustee, Florida where I worked on the construction gang, building a T-Building. Then I was pulled out to go to trial and sentencing in Palatka. I was housed with Sidney Jaffee, who Mike Wallace interviewed on *60 Minutes*. Sid taught me to read corporate annual reports. My court appointed attorney told me I was in luck, for the judge had been in a good mood. The judge gave me only the maximum five years, but not the $5,000 fine.

This particular judge denied the Canadian government's request to allow Sidney Jaffee to do his time in Canada. He told him that he committed his crime in Florida and would do his time in Florida. However, what the judge hadn't figured on was that the bounty hunters who went to get Sidney in Toronto had had no legal authority to do so in Canada. They actually abducted him and brought him across a national boundary. The Canadian government indicted, tried, and convicted the bounty hunters on the abduction charges. They then called the judge in the US about a trade. I never did find out about the outcome of this.

Since I had a new sentence I had to go back through Lake

Butler again, then to Florida State Prison-Butler Transient Unit, and then on to Baker. I had to put in my time in Florida under an alias, as the courts confused my alias with my real name. I took a plumbing class with a great instructor, Edgar Dewey Ford, and my diploma had my name as "Ashton Howard Schwalb," aka Paul Martin. Ashton was my mentally ill brother-in-law. I knew he would never get in trouble if I used his name.

While at Baker I lived through violent riots and also the daily threat of violence. During the first riot, the horn sounded while I was in the yard. We had a few minutes to get inside before they started shooting. I went to my dorm and stood there looking out the jalousie windows at guards stretching out a prisoner and beating him with a baseball bat. Then a guard with a shotgun who was chasing a guy ran toward where I was standing but veered off just in time for his shot to miss the prisoner and shatter the glass right in front of me. I then decided I had seen enough and went back and sat on my bunk!

Back then we were allowed to have real money on our person in prison. Guys would rob new inmates, and one actually killed another guy for sum of less than a dollar. People were routinely raped. On the positive side, staff members were required to put in reports on each of us for our individual parole hearings. These reports included feedback from the housing supervisor, job supervisor, teachers, and others. I was extremely shocked that I earned first parole. However, I had to wait over ninety days for an interstate compact to be approved so that I was able to parole to my parent's home in Virginia.

During my Florida incarceration, two more riots occurred. Additionally, my wife (whom I'd not yet divorced) tried to block my parole from happening. Prior to my being granted parole, she had a boyfriend who was a deputy sheriff. One morning, as he went out to work, someone shot him. The next day, deputies were at Baker questioning me on the event. I told them I had over 1,000 people who could verify my whereabouts when the incident had occurred. What's more, my wife called my counselor saying I had written threatening letters. He asked me about it, and I told him to ask her to produce them. She could not. He then advised me that when I caught the bus from Lake City to Jacksonville on my parole trip, to not venture outside the building during my (short) layover, that I should get across the state line as quickly as possible!

I also had another issue to deal with. Several black guys found out I made parole and were messing with me. They thought I wouldn't retaliate and lose my parole. So I asked my counselor what to do about this. He promised me that as long as I did not kill one of them, I would get to go home. I immediately exited his office and went out in the yard and confronted the guys. They all became silent!

I met some good people in that system in which I must say I was treated fairly. I made some very good friends there, as well. I learned Spanish, as there were Latinos from Central and South America, though mainly there were Cubans and Haitians.

As prisoners in the Florida system did not get paid for work during my incarceration there, I was given $100 gate money (half of which I gave to a buddy of mine) and a bus ticket to my hometown of Lynchburg, Virginia. I had to report to my parole officer, Bill Hughes, within seventy two hours. Nevertheless, I was charged with assault only a few days after my arrival.

Lee Smith, a professional boxer, lived across Park Avenue from my parents, who lived beside Gary Miller's store. He essentially saved me from myself. He talked me into boxing. He trained me, and we exercised with the Seven Hills Boxing Club in the basement of the Hunton Branch YMCA near my old school, Dunbar High School. It was a drug infested area, but the coaches (both named Rucker but unrelated) kept many people out of trouble. Lee did the same for me. He was not only my coach and mentor, but my friend, as well. I loved him and his family.

Lee had me training for twelve rounds in order to fight at the state tournament; I believe it was to be in the Scope Arena in Norfolk, Virginia. At the same time Lee was training for a fight in Atlantic City, New Jersey. While running one day, Lee had a stroke and died a few days later. His death devastated me, as did my father's death sometime later. I never boxed again, but I did maintain contact with Lee's wife, Karol, who, sadly, died in 2013. Lee was blessed with wonderful children, the last of whom, Cavanaugh, was born after his father's death.

My brother, James Jr, moved to Stephenson, Virginia, just north of Winchester on Rt. 11. There came a point in time when he needed a kidney transplant. I had been taking classes at Central Virginia Community College (CVCC) but dropped out to be tested at Georgetown University Hospital to see if I was a match. He soon came to the point that he was going to die, so they sent him home. I moved in with him for a while, but issues with other family members made it impossible for me to stay. He died not long afterward.

I went back to Lynchburg for a while, then to Northern Virginia. I had a different parole officer in Lynchburg who actually tried to violate my parole and lock me up for not paying off my court costs and fines as quickly as she had wanted me to do so. However, the Florida Department of Corrections refused to violate my parole. They told her they would just extend my parole until I paid off the debt. I transferred my parole to Fairfax County, VA, where I had a great parole officer. I eventually met a woman whom I wanted to marry; however, I first had to bring her to see my parole officer and also let her view my criminal record in its entirety. I did this, and she then paid off my court costs and fines. We married and moved to Buena Vista, Virginia, to her hometown. Not long after I moved there, I was released from parole.

My second wife had issues from her past, as did I. She cheated on me not long after we were married. I caught her in our bed asleep with another man. I went out to my truck, got a sledgehammer, and went back inside and woke them up. I put the guy in the hospital for quite some time. Since her family was wealthy and politically connected, I knew I was going to jail. The city cops did come, but after she told them what happened, they told me they did not see where I had done anything wrong. We moved to Lynchburg. I adopted her very young son, who I loved as my own. A few years later we had a daughter, so I will never regret trying to make the marriage work. I was a licensed building contractor and built houses for Jim Walter Homes and other builders. My marriage kept deteriorating, though, and I began to drink. I never had a DUI, but my driver's license kept getting suspended. Then I wrote a couple of bad checks and was given a one year community diversion sentence and one year of probation. I completed the community diversion program and was transferred to regular probation.

For approximately four months, my probation officer refused to see me. Then she called, saying that I had to get to her office right away and threatened to lock me back up for not seeing her. Fortunately for me, I'd been around for a long time and covered my behind. I had phoned often, which was logged on file, and I had gone by the office often, which was logged as well. On each monthly report I had asked why she wouldn't see me and cited the times I had attempted to make contact with her. She had been mad at me because she had (unsuccessfully) tried to force me to commit fraud by signing a document stating that a particular nonprofit had obtained a job for me. They had not done so, and I refused to sign. When I changed jobs, they took my last pay check and refused to give it to me. I embarrassed them all, for I went to the local OSHA office and filed a formal complaint with the Department of Labor and Industry. The probation officer had just been trying to get a little "get back." Only it had failed this time.

There came a point in time when my Post-Traumatic Stress Disorder, or "PTSD," my head injury, my alcoholism and rage, and my wife's continual infidelities combined, created a mixture that was volatile, to say the least. It resulted in my current incarceration. My probation officer compiled my pre-sentence report for the judge and finally exacted her revenge upon me. There were many inaccuracies in the report that were detrimental to me.

I spent a year in jail, and then entered the Virginia Department of Corrections. Thus began my extended journey through prison life.

Chapter 3
Enduring Incarceration

LIFE INSIDE PRISON is stressful for both staff and offenders. It affects all concerned psychologically, emotionally, and physically. However, one is affected long before entering any prison. Imagine yourself, if you can, in the following scenario.

You come home from work and grab a bite to eat. As you are eating, the police come and arrest you. You're taken before a magistrate. She is going to deny you bond, but goes through the motions anyway. You are photographed, fingerprinted, strip searched, and given jail clothes. You are then placed in a cellblock with others. You can actually feel the disdain and disrespect that those in authority have toward you.

Over the next six months you adapt to your situation. You learn that some of the jail staff members are vindictive, spiteful people, and others have little experience in working with people. The most frightening thing is that these persons now control your life. You realize that you've ceased being a regular person, and now you are an inmate, an offender, or whatever term it is that those in authority use to identify you.

You've entered the criminal justice machine and must now be

processed. You enter a courtroom where the clerk reads the charges against you and asks if you understand the charges. You want to scream out, "Hell no, I don't understand any of this," but you simply reply in the affirmative. It is all just a formality anyway. You are then asked, "How do you plead to the charges presented against you, guilty or not guilty?" You state that you are not guilty. This exact situation occurred just after your arrest, and at your preliminary hearing. Now it is happening again, but today is your trial date.

The prosecutor and your attorney select the jury. The prosecutor is truly pleased with this jury—most of the people on the jury are acquaintances or friends of his. One lady is the deputy sheriff's sister. The only person the prosecutor did not seem to have on this jury was his mother!

The evidence is presented, primarily via witness testimony. Your attorney cross-examines the witnesses. Then you are called to the stand to testify. Your lawyer asks you a series of questions, and then the prosecutor cross-examines you.

You realize that none of the folks on the jury constitute a jury of your peers. There are no Native Americans, alcoholics, or convicted felons on the jury. The newly appointed judge gives the jury its instructions, and they go into the adjacent room to deliberate. Court is adjourned until the jury comes back with their verdict. A deputy seats you in a chair right next to the door to the jury room. You can hear most of their deliberations. You hear one woman clearly state that you spoke the truth about one of the charges, but you had lied about the other two. Later she says that if they give you twenty years on one charge, they need to give you twenty on the second and two on the third to make things neat and even!

The jury returns to the courtroom and renders its verdict and recommended sentencing. Your attorney asks that the jury be polled in order to officially enter these data on the transcript (each individual juror's name and verdict). The judge dismisses the jury, thanking them for their services. Court is dismissed, and you are returned to jail.

Later on your lawyer comes to see you and tells you that a friend of one of the jurors told him that most of the people on the jury didn't believe that you were guilty of the second charge—the one for which you may face twenty years. Your lawyer wondered why they hadn't voted that way and was informed that the young lady had been certain of your guilt and very insistent about it, as her own brother was found guilty of a similar crime. Besides, all the jurors were tired and hungry by this point. The sun had set hours before, and they just wanted to go home. They all knew that the police would not have arrested you if you weren't guilty. Right?

Over the next three months you sit around and ponder your fate. In the meantime, there are front page articles in the newspaper telling what a despicable character you are. Sentencing day arrives, and the judge tells you that if it were up to him, he would sentence you to less than the jury's recommendation. But he sincerely declares that he must adhere to their sentencing requests. This is a lie, as any final word on sentencing is up to him, but as a brand new judge, and with all the media attention, he didn't want to make waves. Besides, no one who really matters gives a damn anyway! After sentencing, the deputy who escorts you back to the jail tells you over and over again how sorry he is that this happened to you. Even he knows you just got royally screwed!

You spend another three months dealing with a bitter divorce. You worry about what will happen to your children and if you will be able, at least in some part, to be a father to them. You are exceedingly angry over all this and over the twenty year sentence on the second charge. You wonder who will stand by you while you are in prison. You are suddenly assaulted by many unfamiliar emotions and truly do not know how to deal with them. There are too many unknowns to fathom.

Eventually you are transported to a prison reception center where staff members go through your property, telling you what you can keep and what you must send out. What you do not know is that the offenders working there are notorious thieves and make quite a lot of money stealing new intakes' property and selling it to other offenders. You are given your prison identification number. You are now officially a cog in the criminal justice machine.

If you've never experienced this situation before, you may be feeling shocked and bewildered and trying to find your way. You may hold great dislike for authority figures, especially if you've perceived or experienced any abuse of authority in your past. Two weeks after being transferred to the reception center, you catch the flu from your cell partner but the medical department will not treat you. You phone a family member who in turn phones the prison and attempts to get them to give you medical treatment.

The next thing you know, the assistant warden calls you in and chews you out for having someone call the prison. He doesn't give a damn if you are sick; he just doesn't want to be bothered. You have words with him. He takes you to the medical unit and jokes with the medical staff; "This prisoner thinks he has a fever, but it doesn't make sense because it is only one hundred degrees outside." You tell him that with all the clowns out of work, he should be auditioning for their jobs. He warns you to watch what you say, and this time you respond with a true statement, that you are already in prison and time does not stop, so he should do what he will. The medical staff finally treats you for your illness.

A few weeks later you get called back to medical for the original complaint. A male nurse asks you why you need to be seen. You reply that you do not know why, for you did not request the visit. He becomes very nasty, telling you he has the form (signed by you) requesting treatment. You explain that if he would actually read the whole thing, he would see that you were treated for this illness two weeks beforehand. He then turns red in the face and angrily tells you to leave.

Next you are processed through the medical unit and see a psychologist who tries to put you down in order to anger you, yet the psychologist is easily angered, as well. You see a pleasant counselor who proposes which academic and treatment programs you should take once you are at your assigned prison where you will be transferred in a couple of months. You are again in a brand new environment and must adapt both to it and the people with whom you must now live and interact.

Now think carefully about this scenario, and imagine how you would be feeling at this point, after all that has transpired. What kind of attitude will you have?

All this has greatly impacted your life, but whether you realize it or not, it has impacted your family, friends, and loved ones negatively, as well. You are just beginning to experience the variety of issues that you will eventually encounter within and without prison walls. Corrections propaganda states that its goal is to enable offenders to maintain community and familial ties. However, policy tends to have the opposite effect. Therefore, it is of utmost importance that offenders endeavor to learn quickly how to effectively manage their relationships.

One will encounter many offenders and staff who do not possess critical thinking skills. They easily fall prey to the "rumor of the day", especially if it is something negative about someone. They easily fall in to groupthink and act accordingly. Most of them just want to be accepted and to fit in. These circumstances explain why new gang members are so easily recruited. Potential recruits, especially the younger ones, would rather belong to a group that preys on others than be one of those preyed upon. Some just want to make a name for themselves.

One will encounter people who hold prejudicial and racist views. These beliefs are not limited to Caucasian offenders, but can be observed among minority offenders and staff at large. Many an offender has been traumatized in the past, holding on to feelings of guilt, self-condemnation, and shame. These are extremely touchy individuals, some highly volatile, and they do find it difficult to be forgiving of others, yet harder to forgive themselves. The majority of offenders are greatly concerned with their reputations, though are unaware of the vast difference between reputation and character.

Now imagine being betrayed or possibly abandoned by those you love. Imagine your former spouse fighting you in court so that you can never have a relationship with your own children, and because you are a prisoner courts always deny your pleas for visitation. Imagine your children growing up without you. Now you are a stranger to them. You eventually are imprisoned long enough for your children to become adults who choose to not have any kind of relationship with you. Then imagine being locked up for a couple of decades with close family members dying until there is hardly anyone left—or no one at all. How will all this affect you? Is all lost? Is there any way you can have any kind of life while imprisoned, or after your release?

The answer is yes! However, each person must determine his or her own method for facing personal issues and to determine what is one's purpose in life. One must develop the ability to discern the proper path for life while imprisoned in order to work toward meeting achievable goals post-imprisonment. Institutions offer a variety of programs as stated in my introduction, but unfortunately the quality of instruction or facilitation may at times be poor due to staff incompetence.

There has to be a better way! There is, but it takes political courage in order for elected officials to not only do the right thing but also do what is truly effective. Then it must be acknowledged that staff inside America's prisons, whose background has been mostly with punishment-only criminal justice regimes do not easily adapt to a rehabilitative model, for old habits die hard. Only external credentialed professionals should operate and manage re-entry programs and other treatment programs. Otherwise taxpayers will be throwing good money after bad.

From the reception center I referred to earlier, I was transferred to the general population of the same prison, Powhatan Correctional Center, with several other prisoners. Upon arrival we had our property searched again. Then we were housed in C-1 cellblock. I was placed directly into a general population cell with a cell partner. Shortly afterward, we were taken downstairs to a room where an inmate gave an orientation to the prison. It was all bullshit and of no help at all. As we returned to the cellblock, one of the guys said he bet I did not want to be housed at this particular prison, for it had a violent reputation. He actually looked shocked when I told him that this prison was one of my three choices for placement. The other two choices were fairly violent, as well.

He was a big man and looked tough, but for all his bravado, he was in fact scared. He attempted to use his size to intimidate others in a place where it was not the size of the body that mattered, but the size of the heart. One encounters much false bravado in prison. However, one cannot judge a book by its cover, for some of the most deadly people I've encountered in prison looked like little ninety pound nerdy weaklings! I've witnessed these guys taking down huge power lifters with no problem at all. Inside prison no one can be discounted as a threat to anyone else's safety.

Upon our return to the cellblock I also ran into two fellows who had done time with me in Florida. One of them, an older fellow, still made wine and acted much as he had in Florida. The other, a young fellow, acted more manly and was much louder than he had been in Florida. While I was a bit disoriented, I knew that as a former Marine and having survived those very violent experiences in Florida, I could handle any violence that came my way. However, it was the softer issues that troubled me the most.

I was still naive about many things. One example of my naiveté is back when my buddies at Baker Correctional Institute in Olustee, Florida pulled a very good prank on me. I was in the open shower area shampooing my hair. All of a sudden, I felt a presence near me. I quickly rinsed the shampoo out of my eyes and was shocked by what I saw. A few feet in front of me was a young, naked "gump" bent over with his rear in the air. He turned his head to look at me. He looked me over with a huge smile on his face. I panicked, grabbed my towel, and ran straight out of the shower and in to the dorm where my buddies were waiting. They laughed so hard that tears were streaming down their faces.

Another example occurred about a year later. I was sitting on my bunk inventorying store box items with my friend who had the adjacent bed. His younger brother came and sat by me. The situation was nothing unusual, so I paid no attention to his brother. My friend asked me if I saw anything different about his brother. I looked at his brother and said, "No, I don't see anything different about him." He then told me to look down at the brother's legs. I thought it a strange request but did so. What I saw left me speechless! His brother was wearing a pair of cutoff jeans and had shaved his legs! My friend then began to rant about the fact that he didn't know why his brother did that stuff. Then he laughed and said that "all he screwed was the black guys, and the least he could do was give a white man a shot of ass!" I was truly at a loss for words!

The next event involved the brother and the guy with whom he always bought marijuana, and it just baffled me. The brother and this guy always bought pot together and split the cost. At one point, the brother told the other guy to go get some pot fronted to him and that he would give him his share of the cost later. He did so, and they smoked the pot. Afterward the brother refused to pay for his share. It was a setup! The dealer told the guy that if he didn't pay him, there would either be "shit on his dick or blood on his knife." The guy was scared to death and came to me asking how he could deal with the situation effectively.

I told him to trick the guy by telling him to come to his bed after midnight count, but beforehand to sneak two small weights in the building after dark. When the guy comes to his bed with an erection, I instructed him to take the two weights and slam his penis with them. And then beat the daylights out of him! It would work.

I was listening just after midnight when I heard a loud grunt followed by a series of groans. I thought to myself, "He did it!" The next morning I did not see the guy and thought he had gone to the "hole" for beating the dealer with the weights. I asked a guy whose bunk was next to his if that was what had happened. He told me that no, the guy had not gone to the hole but had gone home. That was a surprise, but what he told me next was even more of a surprise. Instead of attacking the dealer he'd let him have anal sex with him! He did this knowing that he was going home the next morning! All that grunting and groaning turned out to be for a much different reason than I had thought. To me, the guy's actions were truly unfathomable.

So you can see that I needed some schooling on how people act and why they act in the ways that they do. Fortunately for me, old school "Dog" from Petersburg came to population from receiving along with me. He had done time at the Walls in Richmond with some of my relatives in years past. He began to school me on how to read people and situations. Dog had done a lot of time beforehand and had a wealth of knowledge. Over time I got to the point where I could evaluate and analyze people and situations unconsciously. Dog gave me a great gift. Those lessons have served me well from that time onward.

Sometime later I saw an interview with Will Smith, the singer and actor, during which the interviewer asked Smith how he continued to choose good projects in which to act. His reply has stuck with me ever since. He stated that he looked for patterns to help guide him. From this point onward I not only would evaluate and analyze but would also consciously look for patterns, as well, especially behavioral patterns of the people with whom I was compelled to interact.

Prior to this current incarceration, I had the essentials of life. I had a family and a few friends. Even if dysfunctional, my life had purpose. When a person enters prison, he experiences the transformation from a life in which he made his own decisions and chose how to live his life to an environment that inculcates dependence and severely limits choices and opportunities to use decision-making abilities. Unfortunately, prisons are structured and operate in such a manner that offenders become more and more dependent and less and less self-reliant over time.

One can feel afloat and at sea with no safe harbor or anchor. Prison life is hard enough as it is without letting it become wasted time. If one has a purpose in life however, one can survive almost anything. A quote from the philosopher, Friedrich Nietzsche truly illustrates this fact: "He who has a WHY to live for can bear almost any HOW."

Three excellent books also emphasize the previously mentioned fact: *Man's Search for Meaning*, by Dr. Victor Frankl; *Father Arseny*, by Vera Bouteneff; and *The Purpose Driven Life*, by Rick Warren. The first of these books reports the author's experiences in a Nazi concentration camp, while the second reports Father Arseny's experiences as an Orthodox priest in Russian gulags. The last of the three titles helps in defining purpose and finding it in one's life. All are very enlightening reads.

Upon my placement in general population, I was housed with Jeff Smith, a former Navy guy who hailed from Indiana but was stationed in the Tidewater area of Virginia at the time of his arrest. He had been convicted of robbing and assaulting a clerk in a convenience store he frequented almost daily. The clerk's initial description of her attacker was of a clean shaven man. Jeff was arrested within twenty four hours of the attack. His mug shot shows him with a full beard. One can shave a beard within twenty four hours, but one cannot grow one within that same time period. Interestingly enough, after the investigators showed the clerk a photo of Jeff, she changed her description of her attacker to a bearded man!

So here I was with a fresh forty four year sentence, twenty of which I felt was unjustified, and was mad as hell at the world. Conversely, Jeff had four life sentences, all of which were unjustified, and he was all calm, cool, and collected! He kept busy working and participating in sports and various other programs, and he was even a reporter for *The Southside News*, our newspaper. He and other reporters for the newspaper had interviewed people such as Chuck Colson and Joe Gibbs, among others. He provided me with a good example of how one can choose to be positive and productive; even in the worst of times one can find purpose for life.

Jeff invited me to participate in various programs and even allowed me to work on the newspaper. However, the most important thing he did for me was to get me a tutoring position in the prison school with Mr. James Good, an academic instructor. This one act impacted my life positively from that day forward. Mr. Good is a Mennonite whose daily example provided me with a role model to emulate. I worked for him for three years, and he has been a true friend and mentor ever since. He has been retired for quite a few years now, and at the time of this writing tutored international students at Eastern Mennonite University in Harrisonburg, VA, and was on the board of directors for Gemeinschaft Home, a halfway house for adult male offenders.

Jeff transferred away in the mid-1990s. We corresponded for a while, but over time we lost contact with one another. I will be forever grateful for what he did for me. He and Mr. Good helped me find a purpose for my life, even while I was incarcerated. I found that my purpose was to be of service to others, especially in the areas of education and career training.

Even with my newfound purpose, there was still a great void in my life. The greatest regret in my life is the fact that I have not been a father to my children. When first incarcerated, I had no knowledge of my eldest son. My younger son was six years old, and my daughter was just shy of two years in age. For over a decade, I wrote my younger children weekly and petitioned the courts for visitation rights—but it was to no avail. At the first court hearing, the Court Appointed Special Advocate (CASA) volunteer filed her report with the court and testified that she did not feel that a prison visiting room was a proper place for a child to visit. Then she turned to me and said that she did not mean forever, "just not now." The judge agreed with her recommendation, and the "just not now" eventually became "forever."

Early in my prison sentence I was able to telephone my children, but my ex-wife's new husband grabbed the phone from her hands and told me to "call someone who cares." If I could have reached him physically at that moment, I would have showed him how much I cared! Later they tried to terminate my parental rights completely, but I challenged that by filing a judicial complaint against the judge (my ex-wife's lawyer), and he immediately had to recuse himself. The matter was later dropped.

In the CASA report, my younger son stated that he did not want to have anything to do with me. That cut me to my core. They moved to another county, and I filed for visitation with my daughter. My lawyer was able to speak to her. She said she wanted to see me, and been getting all my letters and still had them. The judge ruled that she could see me if she wanted to, but my ex-wife made sure that never happened.

The only way I knew where they were all those years was through a federal law my friend, Terry Brogan, discovered that allowed me to obtain my children's school records. In 1999, while I was on the phone with my best friend Greg Day of New Martinsville, West Virginia, Greg told me I would never believe who had just pulled in his driveway. It was my ex-wife and my younger children. I spoke to my ex-wife and daughter, but my son had run off with Greg's son, Brandon already, and I didn't get to speak with him. When I tried calling later that weekend, they had already left; I felt terrible that I didn't get to speak with my son.

My ex-wife was in the midst of a divorce with her husband, thus the reason for the trip. He must have been very good to my kids, though, for they wanted to remain living with him. I certainly appreciated his being good to them. Brenda, Greg's wife at the time, spent time with my kids, telling them about their father. She did not sugarcoat the story. She told them everything about me—the good and the bad. Most importantly, she let them both know how much I loved them and that I would always love them, no matter what. They took photos of my kids and mailed them to me. I simply treasure those photos. Shortly afterward, my daughter wrote me a letter and another the next week, but then I never heard from her again. I still have those two letters and treasure them, for they are the only letters I've ever received from my kids. That year I was also able to purchase my daughter's school pictures.

Greg and Brenda were always true friends, and I loved them both deeply. A few years earlier, they had driven all the way from New Martinsville, West Virginia on the Ohio River, picking up my mother in Virginia on their way, and visited me on "Family Day." I was working the soda truck with my friend, Jomo, so I was already there when they showed up. It was a very pleasant surprise. True friends can carry you through very difficult times. Unfortunately, Greg died in the recent past. He will always be sorely missed by all who knew him. His extended family essentially adopted me and became my family. They've always been there for me, and I will be there for them. True friends are a treasure during the difficult years of incarceration.

In 1999, I was transferred to a lower security prison. I had spent the last several years living in a very adversarial environment. At my new location I encountered guards whose last job had been bagging groceries—they thought they were tough guys but did not have a clue as to what real toughness was. Soon one got out of line with me, and I was sent to the segregation unit. This event occurred around the same time as the Columbine High School shooting in Colorado. I was later transferred to the segregation unit at another prison, allowed out on the yard for two weeks and then transferred to an adjacent prison that housed higher security level prisoners.

At my new assignment, Buckingham Correctional Center, I encountered many guys who had done a lot of time, and I made many friends. One of these people was "Red," who had been incarcerated for about thirty years. There was a young man there that Red had taken under his wing and made sure no one would mess with him. I thought he looked familiar, but his last name didn't fit. In years past, I had always thought I had a child with a woman who I had loved deeply. I actually searched vital records in several states, but I never found anything under her name. While in the visitation one weekend, I was surprised to see this very woman! She and her sister were visiting this young man. Neither she nor her sister ever spoke to me, although they often glanced in my direction. Many old memories flowed through my mind. I wondered what their relationship was to this young man. As I was thinking, all of the sudden she put her arm around this young fellow. Her eyes locked with mine, and she gave me the most penetrating look. The young man looked very uncomfortable. He never looked at me directly. I knew she was trying to convey a message, but at the time I did not quite get it.

It was a cold day, but after the visit, I went out on the recreation yard to walk. There was a dividing fence separating one side of the yard from the other. There was hardly anyone out. As I walked around the track, part of which paralleled the fence, I saw the young man come down to the lower end of the yard and up to the fence. He stood there as if he were waiting for someone; he never spoke. I walked by him several times before he turned slowly, shoulders sagging and head low, and walked away. He looked so sad. Seeing him like that really bothered me. I thought that whomever he was waiting for had really let him down. What I did not know then was that I was the one who had let him down! It was only after I had transferred to another prison that I learned that he was my son. I learned that he had been placed with a very loving family via an open adoption, which explained the difference in last name. I've repeatedly tried to make contact with him and my other children, but all to no avail.

More recently I used the Social Security Administration's letter forwarding service out of Baltimore in order to contact my children. I did not have my eldest son's social security number, so I had to send a letter to his biological mother. I had the numbers for my other two children, so I could have sent letters directly from the Social Security Administration to their respective places of employment. These were sent months ago, and to date I have received no response from anyone.

Eventually I did find a way to partially fill this void in my life. I sponsored a little boy, Tint Koko, in Myanmar (Burma) through World Vision in December 2000. He was three years old at the time. I have often acted as a father figure to younger prisoners, but since I had some discretionary funds, I figured the sponsorship was a very good way to spend them. I could not do anything for my own kids, but I could make a big difference in the life of someone else's child. I would write him, and a translator in Thailand would translate my letter for him. They censored my letter once when I referred to my Christian faith. At that time, such a reference was a big no-no in Myanmar. He would write me, and once again the translators in Thailand would convert the message, this time into English for me. I received his written letter along with the translated version. Each year I received an update on his education, health, etc., as well as a photograph. He never knew I was a prisoner. I sponsored him for ten years. Then, all of a sudden, my being a prisoner was a problem, and they forced me to drop my sponsorship. He would still be sponsored by the nonprofit, a so-called Christian organization that would not even allow me to write him one last letter saying goodbye, even though the letter would be translated and subject to censorship. After ten years of contact, I felt that it was a very cruel thing to do to me and to him. It truly saddened me then and saddens me still.

From 1994 to 1998 I worked on earning my bachelor's degree via West Virginia University. I also completed two apprenticeships and a vocational class. I completed several institutional treatment programs, as well. In 2002 I earned a master's degree in Construction Management via Heriot-Watt University, Edinburgh, Scotland. During all that time I encouraged others to continue their educations, be it vocationally, academically, or through independent study. I assisted others in every way I could in the furtherance of their education. All those activities gave me a purpose, a reason to get up in the morning.

Over the course of my life, I've experienced many a dark day. However, it has been my faith in the Creator that has carried me through the darkest of times. Too many people miss out on a relationship with Jesus, with someone who knows the absolute worst about us, yet loves us nonetheless. They miss out on being involved with someone who can be trusted totally. This relationship is truly a treasure to have in an environment where trust is almost totally non-existent. They miss out on the understanding that when they try to handle things totally on their own is when things get all messed up. They fear being seen as weak, not realizing that in their weakness should they rely on God, and they will be truly strong. Believe me; it takes more strength to be non-violent in prison than to react with violence. God has a specific plan for each person's life. Each person has a specific purpose that only he or she can fulfill. Any trials, tribulations, and suffering must be viewed as preparatory training for what each person is ultimately meant to do. Each individual must seek his or her specific purpose, the meaning to his or her life.

Many of us are wounded by past experiences. Too many of us allow our past to negatively impact our own present and future. According to Proverbs 23:7, "For as he (man) thinketh in his heart, so is he." In other words, our thoughts give birth to our words; our words give life to our actions. Many of us have been wronged in our lives. If we hold on to these past wrongs and fail to forgive those who have wronged us, it only leads to a life of resentment and bitterness. A life full of bitterness negatively impacts a person emotionally, spiritually, and physically. It produces tension and anxiety both which weaken the body. It also destroys relationships.

Lack of forgiveness means that the injured party reserves the right to get even with or seek revenge on those who wronged him or her. We all know that it is difficult to forgive. However, forgiveness does not require that the act be excused or forgotten, but only that the wronged party gives up the resentment and the right to seek revenge. Forgiveness is not a matter of feelings, but an act of will, a conscious choice. Being unforgiving cripples; forgiveness frees, leading to a full, satisfying life. Forgiveness is not primarily for the benefit of the forgiven, although they do receive benefits from it. Forgiveness is truly for the wronged party being enabled to escape the chains of the past.

Forgiveness is especially difficult when applied to one's self. We all experience guilt at one time or another; it is a normal emotion. People should accept responsibility for things that are under their control. However, they must discern the difference between authentic and false guilt. False guilt stems from accepting responsibility for things beyond one's control. An example can be seen when a child's parents divorce, leading the child to believe the divorce to be his or her own fault.

One's conscience allows feelings of culpability and regret, and this is beneficial as feelings act as a warning sign that one has committed a wrong act or failed to do what he or she should have done. Such feelings work well as long as there is balance. However, it does not take much for imbalance to occur, especially true when it comes to offenders. Whether they know it or not, many offenders feel shame. Shame is essentially a feeling in which people feel a deep sense of lack of acceptance due to wrongs they committed or those committed against them. All offenders have experienced being shamed in court. Prosecutors seek to make defendants appear to be the worst people on earth. Prior to trial, one may have been a decorated war veteran; at trial he or she may be portrayed as a psychopath, a trained killer. Should one happen to be found not guilty of a criminal act, the prosecutor simply states they did not have enough evidence to convict. One is never declared innocent, and the media subscribes to this view. They will publish a series of articles presenting the alleged victim's story—the only story that really seems to matter. Any references to the defendant are of a derogatory and demeaning nature. An overabundance of cop shows exist on television, all posting the disclaimer that "All defendants are presumed innocent until proven guilty in a court of law." Viewers cannot possibly believe this statement to be true, for it is in fact a lie. If it were true, the police could not arrest you and throw you in jail, presumed innocence and all!

Offenders often feel the condemnation of society and of the criminal justice system, and they experience the condemnation of staff on a daily basis, expressed both consciously and unconsciously through tone of voice, speech, and body language. It is made perfectly clear to offenders that they are considered inferior. Staff continuously exhibits an air of superiority and arrogance. Offenders should not feed such delusion however, as staff members are just as fallible as everyone else. Offenders should accept responsibility for things under their control, and when appropriate, they should have regret and feel remorseful. It is not only the right thing to do, but it contributes to their mental health as well. Afterward, if possible, they should try to make amends, and then focus on the future. Offenders should not feel shamed by their pasts. They should accept the past for what it is and attempt to move on. They most definitely should not accept the condemnation of others who do not determine a person's worth—only God determines that. He loves people in the midst of their darkest days and deepest sins. He may hate a person's actions, but never the person. He accepts people where they are, as they are. Like the father in the parable of the prodigal son in the Bible, He patiently and lovingly waits for the lost to come and seek him out.

Offenders must not internalize the judgment and condemnation of others. Self-condemnation is not healthy. Remember: even Job's friends believed that he had done something wrong because he was faced with so much misfortune in such a short period of time. However, Job endured and trusted the Lord. Job knew that God was one of restoration, not condemnation. Feelings of guilt, shame, and condemnation must be addressed. The root cause of these feelings must be identified. It may not be easy, but it is most definitely necessary. While it cannot be resolved overnight, it will never be resolved until one faces it and begins to deal with the issues.

Personally, I am in my fifties now and am just coming to terms with the trauma of my childhood and thereafter. My Cherokee father was abused as a child. He in turn essentially ignored me until I became a teenager. Dad actually resented me for many years because he thought I was not his biological son due to my mother's promiscuity. My mentally ill mother would go on crying binges and beat me until she became too tired to continue. She would often give my meager belongings away. I always felt unprotected with no safe harbor anywhere. There is much more to my story, but suffice it to say that from those years onward, I had real issues originating from those traumatic experiences.

To date these issues have not been fully resolved. Over the years these circumstances brought about much pain in my life and through me to the lives of others. For a couple of decades, prison psychologists essentially told me to "just get over it." Well, I desperately wanted to do so, but I did not know how. The culture of mistrust in prisons affects staff, including mental health professionals. These individuals begin to view offenders as manipulators, and so the former can easily ignore authentic cries for help. If one is fortunate, the prison chaplain (where one is assigned) can be of help, whether one is religious or not. Additionally, they may be able to recommend good self-help books, as can the librarian. Do not discount assistance available from other trustworthy offenders who have experienced and overcome such issues.

Many offenders have been deceived into thinking they are unworthy for most of their lives. They may base this falsehood on how they have been treated in the past or on what has been said of them. They may replay those memories over and over again in their minds. It is all a lie, but until those memories are replaced with others, the deception lives on. Offenders need to search diligently to determine who they truly are and to recognize their true value. They need to discern truth by learning to read between the lines, to perceive readily what is not obvious. Once they can discern truth, obtaining an accurate perception of their environment and interactions with others, they will begin making sound judgments.

This process may be difficult at first. However, it helps if offenders can look past their immediate circumstances in order to avoid becoming discouraged. In times of discouragement it is best to take things one day at a time. The dawning of each new day offers the hope of a new beginning. Religious faith is of tremendous help during such times. If one places his or her hope in God and asks for His help, he or she can rest assured that He will walk with them every step of the way. However, one must "be still and know I am God:" meaning one must be still and listen quietly for God's directions through His Holy Spirit.

Even as a myriad of personal issues are dealt with, one must not get so caught up in it that thoughts of a future are neglected. Each individual must find his or her own way to endure prison life. There will be trials along the way. However, such trials should be viewed as training for a future vocation or purpose in life. It is training today to meet the needs of tomorrow. Trials refine a person's character and serve as a vehicle to bring people closer to God, who in turn instructs individuals through these experiences. One's character is of more importance than one's reputation; only God can truly form one's character.

During the course of my life I have often experienced God turning negative experiences into positive ones. He always meets our needs and stands by His promise never to abandon us. While we may become lonely at times, we are never alone, for He is always with us. God's love is true and eternal; it does not change. It never wavers. It is constant, sure, and ever-present.

Someday is not today. Like marathon runners, our goal is the finish line, but we must set a pace that allows us to endure to the end. As the journey of one thousand miles begins with one step, we must remember that each step is important. If we set many short term goals in the journey to our overall goal, we can build on each success, one after another. On our own, life inside prison is difficult. However, if we lean on God, he will provide assistance.

Throughout my incarceration I have been blessed to have had wonderful friends and mentors. They know the absolute worst about me, yet they have stood by me through thick and thin. One person who has remained a loyal and steadfast friend and mentor is Dr. Robert "Bob" White. Bob has been a foreign language professor at Lynchburg College in Lynchburg, Virginia since 1966. He primarily taught French, not only at Lynchburg College, but in Paris during the summertime. He is fluent in several other languages, as well. Over the course of his life, he has impacted legions of college students positively, as well as numerous prisoners and former prisoners, including me. Sadly, he had to retire in 2012 due to the effects of Parkinson's disease, yet he remains upbeat and grateful for the life he has.

In 1983 I had paroled out of prison to my parents' home in Lynchburg, Virginia. I was blessed to be assigned to a good parole officer, Bill Hughes. He is the one who suggested that I contact a nonprofit that assists former prisoners. It was through this organization that I met Bob, who volunteered there while teaching noncredit courses at the local low-security prison. My first encounter with Bob was during a mock job interview. He was very tough on us, but afterward I did not have much difficulty with job interviews. He took me on a tour of Lynchburg College and allowed me to sit in on one of his classes. He became not only my mentor, but my friend, as well. He helped me to enroll in the local community college, and later I took a semester at Lynchburg College. It was an oasis in the midst of a city of which I had few fond memories.

Lastly, I want to address the issue of abandonment. Many offenders experience this circumstance during the course of their incarceration. I have experienced it in my own life, and it is very difficult, especially when one is abandoned by someone you truly love. Most abandonment issues involve spouses, and this then affects the children. In many cases when a person is first incarcerated, the spouse vows to stand by him or her, truly meaning it. Over time, the difficulties of life combined with a growing loneliness often lead to adultery and ultimately divorce. A particular pattern emerges. At first, it usually involves complaints by the spouse about issues over which the offender has no control, making him or her feel guilty because if they were not incarcerated, those issues could be resolved easily. The spouse may then argue more and more about almost anything. Communication and contact slow until there is a big argument, or it just ceases without explanation. This situation baffles and deeply hurts the offender, as he or she does not understand what is happening. There are warning signs, but they are either missed due to ignorance of them, or they are ignored because the offender did not want to believe that what was happening was, in fact reality. The offender has no control over the situation, only over how to react. The spouse is abandoning the offender no matter what. If one has children, then this becomes a very delicate situation and must be handled as such. The children probably already feel abandoned by the incarcerated parent, so one must do all one can to maintain contact and a relationship with the children.

The following real life example illustrates this issue and how it might be successfully managed. One day an offender in his late twenties came to me and asked to speak with me privately. Someone else had referred him to me. He told me that he had recently received a letter from his wife, also in her late twenties, stating that a male neighbor had befriended her and their little daughter, but he was just a friend. The young husband was told that the neighbor had taken them to the state fair. Again, the wife emphasized that he was only a friend! He asked me what I thought of the situation, and how should he handle it. I told him that what I had to say next might anger him, but that he needed to hear the truth and prepare himself for what lay ahead. He instructed me to go ahead and say what I needed to say. I explained that the neighbor started out as a friend, but in his wife's heart, she already knew that he would soon be more. I told him that the next few months of his life would be very painful, but he must focus on his child, for in the end her welfare was all that mattered. Women might come and go, but a child is yours forever!

I told him that he must do all that he could in order to maintain contact and a relationship with his daughter, including being civil to his adulterous wife. I could see his heart breaking as I told him this, yet he listened attentively. I reiterated that even while he was experiencing his deepest pain that he must concentrate on what was best for his daughter. As time passed and things progressed between the wife and the neighbor, he handled it exceptionally well. Forewarned is forearmed! He remained civil with his "wife," who not only allowed relatives to bring his daughter to see him, but also visited herself. The last I heard several years ago was that he was still maintaining regular contact with her. His daughter is growing up knowing who her daddy is and that he loves her with all his heart. Although I have been wounded deeply by the fact that I have no relationship with my children, my pain and suffering have value, for they allow me to help this young man to maintain a relationship with his little girl. Throughout one's incarceration, one will learn that many of those thought of as loyal, whether family or friend, will abandon you, yet sometimes the least likely people will stand by you. Over time, complete strangers may befriend you. Throughout it all, there is only one constant—God. He will bless you with wonderful relationships, but only if you are open to them. He fills your needs primarily through others.

I have been blessed to have several wonderful people in my own life. These relationships, along with my faith, have helped strengthen me in times of weakness. Many of these wonderful people have been mentioned in other sections of this work. I love them all very much. My anchor, however, is Dr. Ann Paterson who was the director of Regents Bachelor of Arts degree program at West Virginia University when I was enrolled there. She also made it possible for me to earn my master's degree. Without her constant encouragement and support, I would have long ago given up on any kind of a future and also would have acted accordingly. I love her more than mere words can ever express. My Creator loved me so much that he sent her into my life, as he sent all the others who mean so very much to me.

Do not be deceived into believing that your imperfections and brokenness preclude Jesus from loving you. Jesus was broken for your sake and mine. Too often we allow our personal experiences to affect how we see the world. They shape our worldview. Unconsciously, our worldview, shaped by negative experiences and our brokenness, places limits on Jesus. These limits seem to make no sense, for how does a human being place any kind of limit upon God? It is impossible. These limits are, in fact, limits on how we perceive Jesus. Such perceptions are truly based on how we think

Jesus perceives us, not in how He actually sees us. Take a little time to read the Gospel stories of how Jesus interacted with people. If possible, purchase a copy of the book entitled *Beautiful Outlaw* by John Eldredge. This book explores the personality of Jesus and much more. It will truly transform your view of Jesus and your relationship with Him. The book is a blessing.

Even though I am a very sinful man, my merciful Creator loves me daily and deeply. His Holy Spirit inhabits my being. It counsels me and assists me in my attempt to be a better man today than I was yesterday. Even when I fail at this endeavor—and I fail quite often—Jesus loves me. I pray daily that despite my many weaknesses and character flaws as that he will use me to draw others close to Him. His presence, ever abiding love, and His mercy have enabled me to survive many a dark day in life.

There have been days so difficult that I felt like reverting to my natural instincts and hurting someone. During a six months period when I endured psychological torture, my fellow prisoner and friend Paul truly helped me to get by: day by day. He was a true friend during one of the most difficult times in my life—a story that will be told in a later chapter.

For many years I have been influenced positively by Mennonites like Mr. James Good and Mrs. Ruth Horst, to pursue peace instead of violence, and believe me, peace is more difficult to achieve when living in a violent environment wherein your first, natural instinct is to just hurt someone. Additionally, the writings of Dr. Gerald Schlabach, Dr. Stanley Hauerwas, and Charles Stanley have greatly influenced me. While Catholic, I know I can learn from those of other denominations or faith traditions. (An excellent book on the history of Judaism, Christianity, and Islam is entitled, *The History of God,* by Karen Armstrong.

Relationships and God are what have carried me through all these years of incarceration. Doing "time" is not for the faint of heart. Do not let pride trick you into thinking you can do it all alone. We need others in our lives if for no other purpose than to remind us of our humanity and that there is much more to life than our current circumstances.

I hope that this chapter is helpful to those who are incarcerated and to those who are blissfully but unfortunately unaware of the humanity of the incarcerated. We are fathers, mothers, sons, and daughters, brothers and sisters. All of us are not violent predators as we've been called by politicians in the past. We are real people with real feelings. Yes, we need to pay the price for the wrongs we've committed, but once that payment is complete, there should be a process to restore us as productive citizens in the communities in which we live.

Chapter 4
Types of Offenders

DEPENDING ON WHAT area of the country in which a person is incarcerated, he or she will come in to contact with people from a variety of cultures, nations, languages, and religions. Even if that is not the case in a particular situation, one will encounter and must deal with varied personalities.

As in free society, prison society contains individuals who identify with and act in on certain psycho-sociological roles. The prison identity one assumes or is given by default or due to circumstances may not be anywhere near the one with which the individual identified prior to his or her incarceration.

The primary rule in prison is to mind own your business; however, that rule in more recent times has been violated on a large scale. Even if you mind your business, as a prisoner you need to be aware of your surroundings and the people you must live with. As much as possible you should strive to keep your mouth shut and your eyes open. The ability to observe and recognize patterns of behavior will be a prisoner's greatest asset in navigating prison life. While there are many good and decent people incarcerated, there are some who are just the opposite.

I truly believe that even those considered the worst have some good in them, and thus the capacity for positive change. However, one must deal with them as they are, not as they could be at some time in the future.

Below, I include and discuss many of the roles I have witnessed people assume while incarcerated. This is not an all-inclusive list, and please know that individuals can and do assume more than one role at a time or change roles over the course of their imprisonment. Some of the roles people play are as follows.

EXPERTS

These are the folks who take great pride in being the best at something or having the most knowledge about various subjects, or, in some cases, all subjects. This includes but is not limited to those who are or presume to be experts in: chess, cards, sports, law, religion, or almost any other subject one can think of.

Some may in fact be experts, but most are not. Some are humble, while most are not. Some only seek to share their expertise, while others like to lord it over the less competent. There is an old saying: A little bit of knowledge is a dangerous thing. The meaning of this saying is that if one has only partial knowledge, he or she is a danger to one's self and others.

JAILHOUSE LAWYERS

A true jailhouse lawyer probably knows more about criminal and habeas corpus law than most any practicing attorney. They can be very helpful; however there are many who just deceive people in order to take their money. The following is a true example.

A middle-aged fellow transferred to an old prison I was housed in during the 1990s. He convinced a lot of people that he could get them back in to court to reduce their sentences. This was the first lie even if it was based on fact. By filing a writ of habeas corpus one is essentially back in court; however, the vast majority of those filed are denied by the court. This guy was from another state, and we were in a fairly violent prison. All of a sudden the staff packed him up and transferred him off the compound. We all know it was a strange thing to do. Then the courts started sending back all the habeas corpus writs he had filed on behalf of others. All were denied!

Some of the people he had filed writs for had life sentences. He had offered them hope where none was available. They all came to me to see if I could help them with their writs. I asked for copies of the original writs and read them all. They all were essentially page after page of continuous writing of repeated statements over and over again. In essence it was one long paragraph that went on for approximately twenty to thirty pages. Sadly, I had to explain that while I wanted to help them, it was impossible due to the incompetence of the writ writer. I am glad the guy was transferred off the compound, for he would have been killed if not. He had offered them hope, taken their money, and totally deceived them.

Another example illustrates how a person truly wants to be helpful, but due to unforeseen circumstances his actions end up precluding any further court challenges: A man who had a life sentence came to ask me if a writ of habeas corpus could be filed for him. I told him I needed a copy of all his previous legal filings to review. These filings included a letter from the trial attorney stating that all direct appeals in the state court had been filed and ruled upon. It turns out the time period allowed to file those direct appeals had long since expired in this case. But this was contrary to what the lawyer had stated in his letter, which gave evidence that the lawyer had lied! This brought about a "procedural bar" blocking any further court action on the appellant's part.

The point is that one must be careful. Some people are very competent; some are crooks, while others, like me, can fail even having the best of intentions. What happened bothers me to this day. I never dealt with any criminal law cases ever again. The man whom I tried to help, a close friend, did not hold it against me at all, though. He told me that I was the only one who would even attempt to help him. And it was the attorney who had lied, not something one would expect, especially in writing. Sadly, many years later my friend died in that very same prison.

REPAIR MEN

These are the people who make money by fixing electronic items such as radios, cassette players, CD players, and televisions. Some can fix watches, as well. Many do this as a hustle, but few are truly competent. Prior to using their services, one must check around to see how past customers rate a person's competence, and, most importantly, his trustworthiness. Some of them will "fix" items so they will break down again so you have to pay them more money.

ACQUISITIONS SPECIALISTS

These are the people who can obtain for a fee almost anything you desire. The key thing here is to make sure the item is not stolen from another prisoner. Additionally, some people sell items but must report them stolen in order to be allowed to replace them later. If that happens, you lose the items, your money, and possibly receive some type of punishment. Some will even sell you an item like a television, take your money, then report it stolen so they get it back and you go to the "hole". Like anything else, one must be careful who one deals with. Others deal only with items they have access to in their jobs such as maintenance, the kitchen, or one of the enterprise shops like the print shop. These people do this to supplement their prison wages.

THIEVES AND ROBBERS

Thieves will steal from people on the sly. They look for opportunities to take someone else's property without being noticed. Even items of little value will be stolen by these folks. Some just have to steal. The following incident illustrates how opportunistic they can be.

Late one evening a guy went out of the cell at the hourly door break to get some hot water for a cup of coffee. He was out of the cell no more than five to ten minutes. Meanwhile, his cell partner was lying on the top bunk asleep.

While the door was open a thief sneaked in and moved several newspapers and a pair of jeans that were sitting on a bag of commissary food items. He laid the newspapers and jeans neatly on one of the two stools by the cell table the bag was sitting under, grabbed the commissary bag, and exited the cell. The guy discovered the theft as soon as he returned to the cell with his hot water.

Another example shows how inmates work together. In the mid-1990s a new prisoner's television gets stolen. A "friendly" guy comes around and tells him he will help him get his television back. The "friendly guy" leaves and returns, telling the owner of the television that for a set dollar amount of commissary he can get the television back for him.

The new guy asks an old timer for advice on what to do about his television. The old timer tells him that the "friendly" guy is in on the theft and for him not to give him anything except a good beat down. The television owner does not listen and pays to get his television back. He is told the television is in a bag in a clothes dryer. He hurries to retrieve his television but all that is in the bag is a lot of old newspapers. This guy actually fell for this trick twice before he finally caught on that he would never see his television again. He should have listened to the old timer.

While thieves seek out the naïve and oblivious, robbers seek out the fearful and those easily intimidated. They usually work with one or more partners and often strike in secluded areas like cells and stairwells. Most robbers do not want to hurt anyone. They just want to get the goods and go. I have more respect for them than I do for thieves. Thieves are cowards and will steal from anyone, even people who have looked out for their best interests. At least robbers come to a person face to face and give the target an opportunity to fight back.

COLLABORATORS AND INMATE AUXILIARY POLICE

These folks are some of the slimiest, low down people inside America's prisons. Most would testify against their own mother if it benefitted them. One individual I know did exactly this, testifying against his mother in federal court in exchange for a reduction in his prison sentences!

Inside prison most people start out as collaborators, and others end up as collaborators because they are groomed by staff to be so. They are told that they are not like all those other people with whom they are locked up, that they only made a mistake which anyone could have done. The staff grooms them by doing favors for them and attempting to make them feel special.

Other collaborators choose the role of their own volition, because they wish to manipulate staff. They seek prison jobs that allow them freedom of movement and seek to become indispensable in doing these jobs. They seek to attach themselves to staff who either have power or will be promoted to positions of higher level authority. They either remain collaborators or begin the transition to becoming inmate auxiliary police (AP), informing on anyone and everyone.

Once they transition to AP's and have full access to those in power, they become a menace to staff and offenders, alike. The vast majority of these folks are homosexuals, closeted or not. Their egos expand exponentially; this becomes especially so as they get closer to upper level prison management. Most eventually get to the point where they confuse access to power with holding and wielding authentic power themselves.

Over time their outsized egos and corresponding actions result in the making of numerous enemies, staff, and offenders alike. Eventually, there comes a point in time when they become more a liability than an asset to those to whom they have attached themselves. At this point the staff members will pull the rug out from under the AP and essentially feed them to the wolves. Then all those who they have informed on and mistreated can take their revenge without facing any severe consequences.

There exists a particular pattern to these things. Again, observation and situational awareness will assist offenders and staff alike in identifying these people and in any dealings with them. One such person in Virginia got into a knife fight with another offender over a female guard. The guard had tried to cover up for the AP as she was working the building's lower control room where the knife fight occurred. The other guy went to the hole for a month and was transferred to a higher security level prison. The AP however, spent thirty days in the hole and was released back into population, all the while keeping his institutional job, and had the captain move another guy out of his old cell so he could move back in.

In Florida, an AP at Raiford Prison saved a guard's life during a riot. FDOC rewarded him by making him a guard at Lake Butler Reception Center. He did have a natural life sentence but then was allowed to live in the local community and travel within a limited area. He was a low life who repeatedly would harass and assault offenders who were at Lake Butler or came there for medical treatment. He was especially violent with offenders who came there from Raiford. I must say that when such assaults occurred all the offenders were handcuffed. You see, this is how cowards operate.

The AP can go anywhere inside the prison any time he wants to. He is always ready with a faux smile and a pat on the back. He gets caught having sex, and there are no negative consequences for him or his partner, who also is an AP.

A female guard, much like Tyler Perry's lead character in his movies, has attached herself to an AP in hopes of securing a promotion. The two constantly harass workers within the building and threaten the loss of their jobs if they do not participate in the AP's obsessive compulsive disorder of constantly cleaning. Most of these guys do not have any outside source of funds and need the little pay their prison job affords.

The typical AP kisses up to the staff right until the moment he does not get his way, then he acts like the petulant child he is. Sadly, many others have fallen under his spell and contribute to his dysfunction. Some have become APs themselves. This offender has confused access to power with holding power himself. Eventually there came a point in time when he became an albatross around the neck of his protectors, and they sacrificed him. The AP's always seem to either not know or forget that when push comes to shove, staff will sacrifice them in order to save themselves.

Some years ago, one individual walked around prison like he was the warden. He thought he was untouchable. His ego betrayed him, and he eventually became a liability to the powers that be. When a new maximum security level prison was opened, he was packed up and put on the bus. Others on the bus describe his cries to the guards to see the warden, for there must be some kind of mistake. The guards explained that there was no mistake and that it was the warden who had him transferred! Needless to say, due to his past actions, no one, guards and offenders alike, had any sympathy for his plight. A few actually experienced extreme pleasure at his sudden discomfort and abandonment by his protectors.

POSERS

These are the folks who are always trying to be something that they are not; albeit a tough guy, a convict, or a baller or shot-caller. They all seem to have a tendency to confuse the volume and quantity of speech with substance. The sorry thing is that many offenders and staff alike are fooled by these types of individuals on a regular basis.

Their "tell," or give-away, is this: if a prisoner continuously speaks about being something, it is a pretty sure bet that he is not that of which he speaks. If he is truly all that he claims to be, he need not speak of it, for his actions would tell the tale.

An example of this type of person is the one who constantly brags on all the money, homes, cars, and women he had prior to his incarceration, but seconds later would ask to borrow some inexpensive item, like a hand rolled cigarette (a "roll up"). Imagine that, a millionaire bumming a roll up!

Those who constantly state they are convicts do so meaning that other offenders can trust them, however if they have to continuously say it, they must not believe it themselves! Posers are usually loud and obnoxious. They inform on others to staff in order to be able to get by with all the dirt they are doing. Over the years I've witnessed staff allowing them to violate rules at will and even to indulge in illegal activities—that is, as long as they keep the information about others inmates flowing.

If posers slip up and slack on informing on others, security will come and shake them down, for they usually have many contraband items and even illegal substances. Security does this to put pressure on them, which quickly results in the posers informing on someone. They are not exactly like collaborators or inmate auxiliary police, for they only inform on others to keep getting by with their own activities that violate the rules and often the law; however, like the others previously mentioned, posers cannot be trusted.

They've even been known to have placed illegal substances under others' beds (knives, dope, etc.) or in their living area so as not to get busted with it themselves. They hold no concern for others, even if their actions could result in an innocent person being placed in the hole or receiving a street charge and possibly getting more prison time. Remember that no one inside prison—I mean absolutely no one (staff, prisoners, etc.)—can be counted on to be what they appear to be. One old saying fits posers very well: "You can be whatever you want to be in the penitentiary."

The Mentally Ill and Those with Behavioral Disorders

Prisons have increasingly become dumping grounds for the mentally ill. Prison systems are not equipped to deal with the mentally ill, and sadly the mentally ill cannot access the care they truly need. When placed in general population with other prisoners they are often either victims or violent and disruptive. Some are so medicated that they can barely function. One truly feels for these poor souls.

One of them is a decorated Vietnam War Army Veteran who has been incarcerated for over thirty years and suffers from PTSD (Post-traumatic Stress Disorder). He has visibly deteriorated over time, still denying the care he so sorely needs. The Veterans Administration (VA) has done nothing to assist incarcerated veterans, except to talk a lot, but their speech does not match their actions, or in this case their lack of action. Unfortunately the VA lacks integrity as regards its core mission.

Non-veterans are being denied proper care, as well as are veterans. There needs to be a better way to deal with mentally ill offenders than currently exists; not only for their benefit but for society's benefit and for economic reasons. One thing is for sure: they do not belong in general population with other prisoners who either take advantage of them or are not very understanding in the event they become violent or disruptive.

There are many offenders who develop behavioral disorders over the course of their incarceration. Some develop an obsessive-compulsive disorder and an aversion to germs. Those who live in cells continuously clean them and must have everything in its proper place. They often will not allow anyone to wear shoes inside the cell. While working in maintenance once I needed to change a light bulb in a cell. The guy told me I had to take my boots off prior to entering his cell! I simply turned around and walked away.

One fellow continuously ran water in his cell and constantly stole others' laundry. Once he was sent to the hole for some violation and security pulled out thirteen laundry bags full of other peoples' clothes from his cell. Another fellow would count his cookies and eat a specific number at a specific time each day. If items in the cell were not in their exact location, even a half inch out of place, he had to make sure the items in question were returned to their places. Another offender would constantly inventory his property, all during the day and even in the middle of the night.

These actions are disruptive in cell blocks but more so in open dormitories. They can really get on a person's nerves. One such individual, an AP who has obsessive-compulsive disorder, constantly cleaned the dormitory. He told on so many people to upper management, the house man (whose job it actually is to clean the dormitory) had to fall in line with his disorder or risk being fired. He had free range of the prison and even the staff feared crossing him. He always acted very courteous with a really faux smile, but the moment he did not get his way he would act like a spoiled brat.

The warden and other upper-level management enabled this guy to indulge in his obsession. My belief is that they did him a great disservice, for how will he be able to function out in society, if at all?

Storebox Men

Prisons run stores called commissaries or canteens. In between days when an offender can purchase items from the canteen, one can buy items from the storebox, maintained by inmates. And for times when one must wait for pay for prison jobs, or funds to be sent in from outside the prison, one can borrow items for a short period of time. They all charge interest on items sold. The going rate has been two items borrowed repaid with three items returned (2 for 3). That is, for every dollar borrowed, one pays a dollar and a half back. There are those who are greedy and charge double, that is one for two. Most people stay away from those folks, for their greed is evident, and they are not to be trusted.

Some storebox men have been at it for a long time, others not too long. It is best to deal with established storeboxes, for the new guys often have a lot of drama with them and will work the customer to death on paying the bill. The established guys only address the issue once the customer has missed a payment. Depending on the prison and storebox man, a non-payment can result in serious injury.

Storeboxes provide a valuable service, however, especially in prisons where population goes to the canteen only twice a month, if that often. Some prison administrations don't mind them as long as there is no trouble associated with them. Others do their best to shut them down. They usually sell food items (soups, chips, sweets, etc.), and sodas and coffee, among other items. If one deals with a storebox, it is best to deal with a reputable one, much like one would do with a business out in society. All one has to do is ask around, and other offenders will quickly let one know who to deal with and who not to.

Storeboxes can be utilized, but one must be disciplined in order to not go into debt. Some guys borrow so much that on each canteen day they pay most of their canteen order to the storebox, run out of things, and borrow again. It can be a never ending cycle of scarcity and debt. This must be avoided at all costs. This is especially true pertaining to young prisoners who, in order to pay off their debts may be forced into illegal activities or homosexual acts.

GAMBLING POOL MEN

These are the folks who set up gambling pools primarily via tickets to bet on sporting events. It can be such that one must pick ten games out of 12 or more, or they pick 3, pick 4, etc. There have been better odds, but like anything else involved in gambling, there is no such thing as a sure thing.

The "pick 10s" pay out to any winners from the combined bets placed by participants. The Pool Man takes a cut of the pool for his expenses (he makes the tickets, pays runners to pass them out, and profits). The "pick 3s," "pick 4s," and so on have payouts well beyond what is bet and the pool man must make up the difference if he gets hit (someone wins their bet). However, if no one hits he makes a tremendous amount of money.

These guys research the betting line on all sports and place odds in their favor. From this they determine which games to put on the tickets and at what odds. It really takes a lot of time and effort, but the pay can be good.

As with any business, there are good and decent people; yes, even in prison. But others cannot be trusted. Those who cannot be trusted will try not to pay out when bettors win, or as the 'inside' term goes: put some shit in the game. However, word gets around quickly, and those who do not pay out do not stay in business long. Depending on the prison, they may be putting their lives in jeopardy.

Some prison administrators overlook the activity as long as there is no trouble concerning pools. Others do not like it and come down hard on those involved. Mostly it is harmless fun. Games are more enjoyable to watch if one has even a very small bet placed on them. There are not too many activities that one can enjoy in prison that are not harmful. However, some people have a gambling problem, and this activity is not good for them. Otherwise, it can be a harmless way to spend some time.

CHEFS

These people can take ordinary canteen food items and make

wonderful meals and cakes. And if they obtain items from the prison kitchen they can truly create masterpieces. Some have specialties like making apple pies, and others can cook just about anything. Some do it for fun while others do it to sell their products. Some cook for others for a portion of the items cooked. They can be fairly creative. In days gone by, they even cooked by tying food items in coffee bags to the heating pipes. Now with microwaves available they really can produce wonderful meals.

They help facilitate bonding among offenders who pitch in items to create communal meals with their friends. In these instances all assist in preparing the meal. At times it appears very ritualistic. It seems they enjoy the making of the meal almost as much as the meal itself.

ARTISTS AND ARTISANS

There are many very creative people incarcerated. Some are painters; others draw portraits and create works from wood and leather, and some do glasswork and silverwork. Some of the craftsmen can essentially make anything out of common items. As the old saying goes, "necessity is the mother of invention". This is true. These folks are the ones who do the inventing. They enjoy tinkering and being presented new and even odd challenges. Many produce their works for sale. Others are commissioned to produce portraits or other items. These folks can be temperamental, which is to be expected, but it is only a negative when egos expand beyond talents. Otherwise these are enjoyable persons with whom to associate and do business.

INFORMATION SPECIALISTS

These people, through various means, seem to always have the inside scoop on what is going on within the prison. This includes issues involving the staff and management. Some are collaborators and inmate auxiliary police, while others are not. One must be careful not to listen to a "Bad Scoop Bob," or a person who offers up information that never turns out to be true!

Information is power, especially inside prisons. However, one must be very wary of these folks just as a matter of self-preservation. If information is someone's business, rest assured that he or she is probably gathering information on you. One must be very cautious about relaying information from information specialists to others.

Good intentions aside, one must recognize that people inside prisons live their lives on many levels and present a façade to others. No one truly knows another or his or her intentions. Again, it is best to sit back, observe, and watch for patterns of behavior or existing patterns being broken before speaking or acting on information obtained via information specialists.

DEALERS AND ADDICTS

Dealers deal drugs, and now that tobacco has been banned, they make a lot of money off of having it smuggled into prisons, as well as drugs. They also use the smuggling pipeline to bring in cell phones and other banned items.

Contrary to popular belief, the vast majority of drugs and contraband smuggling inside America's prisons involves staff. They either bring it in directly or turn a blind eye to those who do. In one situation in a prison industry, one staff member, had drugs packed and shipped in by an employee of one of their suppliers. When the supplies entered the prison, the guards searched the shipment as usual but did not break the shipment all the way down. Once the supplies got to the industry location, this staff member, knowing which box contained the drugs, took it in the office under the pretense of checking something out and then took out the drugs and hid them.

All the while, he was trying to place suspicion onto his boss, coworkers, and certain prisoners. Amazingly, the institutional investigator thought he was trying to help catch drug dealers, for along with the guard who worked at the shop, he was always trying to catch others doing something wrong. At the same time, a guard working in population was a major drug seller. No one liked him, for he treated offenders and staff badly. For both of these folks, being assholes was their natural cover.

In many prisons there are many small time dealers who are just trying to make a dollar and possibly get high for free. While many of their customers do fine, those who "shoot up" or inject drugs stand a chance of overdosing. More than a few have overdosed and died. Marijuana is often overlooked and rightly so. No one ever smoked a joint and tried to hurt someone. A person cannot overdose on it. The primary behavioral side effect is having "the munchies." Conversely, alcohol is an issue administrators take seriously, primarily due to behavioral problems of those who are intoxicated. This is especially so when violence comes into play.

Addicts come in all forms. Surprisingly, there are staff who are heroin and crack addicts. One guard, a crack addict, had been in rehabilitation treatment programs several times yet still attained the rank of lieutenant! One counselor was a heroin addict who shot up frequently.

The best advice concerning interacting with dealers and addicts is to not participate in their activities and limit contact with them. No matter how decent some of them may be, many are not. Sooner or later trouble will come knocking.

There are many temptations within prisons. The drug life is one of them. Offenders often begin this activity to seek peace and get a break from the harshness of their environment. In the end it does more damage than good. Offenders cannot fill a void in their lives with drugs, for it is only a temporary fix. The only long term solution comes from the Creator.

GANGS

Prisons today are full of gangs, whether it be Bloods, Crips, MS13, or others. In and of itself, this is not necessarily a negative thing. If the gangs have leaders who have leadership skills and instill discipline into members, there aren't too many problems. Conversely, if there are leaders who don't have a clue of how to lead and don't maintain discipline, everything quickly goes south.

This is also true when there is a leadership vacuum. In such instances, different "sets" within the same gang will attempt to gain control. These actions result in a miniature civil war between gang members at the same prison.

In some prisons, gangs are hardcore, and there can be quite a bit of violence between separate gangs. In other prisons, the gang leaders and members spend a lot of time in the investigator's office telling on others. They recruit heavily inside America's prisons, and the quality of their prospective members is suspect. And this is their weakest link.

Some gangs, when they have a beef with another gang, set up a place and time to battle. In the weaker prisons, they just stare each other down with no action taken whatsoever.

The smartest move when dealing with gangs is to adhere to the primary rule in prison, which is to mind one's own business. It is best not to join a gang if one is independently minded: Once a person is a member, he or she must follow orders, whether in agreement or not. One person was beaten to death by his fellow gang members for disobeying the leadership's orders.

There are people who are classified as associates or "hangers on" by prison officials, who believe these individuals represent the same security risks as gang members. They will be targeted by staff if there is an issue with a particular gang.

One can be friendly to gangs without being an associate or hanger on. The temptation to join a gang is great for those who are scared or weak. Being a member affords them protection. This is why in years past many offenders became Muslims, for the latter protected their own. However, once a person joins an organization, he or she is subject to its rules. It is much better to be independent.

THE RELIGIOUS

One encounters members of various religions inside prison. Some are nothing more than a gang or cult with a religious identification. Others members of are legitimate of religious institutions. Religion can be a very positive aspect of offenders' lives, whether the faith be Wicca, Islam, Moorish Science Temple, Buddhism, or Christianity. Research shows that true adherents of particular faiths and traditions rarely reoffend and return to prison.

What one must watch out for is those who are religious and/ or cultural warriors. These folks act "holier than thou" and cause much conflict within their faith traditions and without. In prisons, if those within one's faith traditions do not believe exactly the same or do not interpret their sacred texts and teachings in the same manner, one deems those folks as enemies and seeks to have them removed. Some have even started fights with fellow believers directly after their services or meetings. They then sought to ostracize their "enemies". These individuals fear interaction with those of other faith traditions and seek to argue and debate with them. One such person remarked that he "would take the Holy Koran and kick Christians' asses with it."

The irony of it all is that some misinterprets his or her own sacred texts and teachings. Again, a little bit of knowledge can be a very dangerous thing. With these "warriors" it most certainly is. If one is secure in one's faith, there is no need to fear anyone else's beliefs. I cannot find anywhere in any faith tradition that is not gang-like or a cult where one must view other human beings as enemies.

Religious beliefs can be debated if done with respect and dignity. However, if confronted by any of these folks, one must refuse to be drawn into a debate, for all the others want to do is argue and prove their points. They will not hear one's point of view. Respectfully, one must tell them there is no need for debate, for everyone is entitled to their own beliefs, that one respects theirs and hopes his or her own will be respected as well.

GUNNERS

These are sick individuals who are morally deficient and lack self-control. In times past, to "gun" someone down in prison meant to stab them. Today this has a totally different meaning. Now it refers to an offender masturbating while a female staff member is within sight. They do it in showers and behind cell doors, and the truly sick will do it almost anywhere, even at church services.

One person was so sick that security told him that if they even caught him with his hands in his pockets they would lock him up. A group of gunners got into an argument over their schedule for gunning the female guard in the control room. They actually established time blocks for this! This was in the 1990s. Now it is much worse, and they see nothing wrong with it since many female staff members cooperate in the sickening behavior.

Much like they do with homosexuality, nowadays, prison officials either turn a blind eye to it, or else they advocate it as a behavioral tool. The thinking must be that if prisoners have their hands full, they will not be fighting one another! However, one must ask the question, if they cannot control themselves inside, with limited access to females, how will they act out in society?"

GUMPS

"Gump" is but one of many nicknames for homosexuals. No matter how good and decent one of these folks may be, inside prison trouble always follows them. Some of it is of their own making because they like a lot of attention and drama in their lives. Some of it is because of feelings others have about them. There have been knife fights over gumps, and people have been killed, as well. One young fellow in the early 1990s was killed because as a barber, he had scissors, and another guy wanted use them to go outside on the recreation yard and kill his gump and another guy who was trying to draw the gump away from him. During the resulting struggle, the barber was stabbed in the chest and died shortly thereafter. Sadly, he was very close to being able to go home.

Some gumps are feminine, while others are macho and actually live under the delusion they are not gay since they are the "man" in the relationship. One will even encounter males with breasts. The most dangerous of them all is the "bootie bandit." These individuals will cajole weaker, often younger males into a friendship and sex, but they will rape another offender if nonviolent methods are not successful.

In one Florida prison in the early 1980s, two older offenders and a younger, newer one were cleaning the kitchen after supper. The two older guys got the younger guy high, even to the point that he passed out. Then they took turns raping him. Afterward, with him lying on his face, pants pulled down, buttocks showing, they took a water hose and hosed him down. Then they left the kitchen. Once the staff discovered the guy laid out like that, they knew the only other people in that area at the time were these two fellows, and street charges were pressed. Both of the attackers only had a few years left prior to going home. They were convicted and given longer prison sentences. Also in Florida, during a prison riot, one young man took advantage of the opportunity to attack the leader of a group of people who were trying to rape him. They had continuously told him what they planned to do. Needless to say, after the riot no one messed with that young man again.

Many of the victims of booty bandits are afraid of reporting the incidents out of shame. An outside group has fought in court to require prison systems to be more proactive in preventing such occurrences. A part of this is an educational program where new prisoners are warned and shown methods people use to take advantage of others.

THE STATE STRUCK

This is usually where an offender has a job and comes to think of it and all those involved with it as his or her personal territory. This can also be true concerning one's relationship with staff. These people actually begin to identify with staff to such an extent that it surpasses the Stockholm syndrome. Some actually believe they are staff. Once they believe this, others must realize they will act as such and cannot be trusted. Limit contact with these folks.

HATERS (COMPLAINERS)

These offenders cannot stand to see others do well. They are constantly jealous of others who may have a better prison job, more money, more friends, etc. As long as others are slightly below them, there is no problem. However, if others are equal to or surpass them in any area, the jealousy begins: the hatred commences, and they seek to undermine those they've targeted. They are gossips and backstabbers. They are also constant complainers, which helps in identifying them.

THE TIMID AND COWARDLY

They are as the heading suggests. They are dangerous, for they seek others to protect them. However, once pressure is applied, they will quickly turn on their friends and protectors. They cannot be trusted. However, some offenders, especially those new to prison are just nervous. The test which was used in Florida's prisons was such that if one was challenged and a guy at least tried to take up for himself, others would not let him get hurt. On the other hand, if upon being challenged a guy folded, no one would have anything to do with him. It is all about heart; if one at least tried to defend himself—even if he lost in that effort—he still gained respect.

QUIET LONERS

These people stay to themselves and mind their own business. They limit contact with others. They are primarily friendly and polite. However, if crossed, they usually are the most dangerous people in the prison. Like the Marine Corps motto goes, they can be your best friend or worst enemy. Others' actions toward them determine which it will be.

HUSTLERS AND CONS

A hustler is just trying to conduct business and earn a dollar. A con is trying to obtain a dollar by cheating others. Many hustlers are trustworthy. Cons are never trustworthy. Only by observation and awareness can one tell the difference between the two.

CELLYS

In prisons consisting of cells, the "celly" is the most important relationship inside. A good celly can make all the difference in the world. Even if all else is terrible in the prison, a good celly gives one an area to get away from it all by giving reciprocal private time in the cell and actually working together to make life a little easier.

Chapter 5
Troubling Times/Signs of Hope

MOST PEOPLE ASSUME that the staff within the criminal justice system is composed of professionals that act as such. That would be an inaccurate assumption for correctional systems are staffed by flawed human beings, as is true in all other parts of society. However, it is my conclusion that a common worldview dominates their thinking, and thus their behavior. It has been my experience that this worldview consists of all the following beliefs:

1. All offenders are ignorant, ill-educated, and have no life successes prior to their incarceration.

2. Staff members are superior to offenders in every possible way; they are more intelligent, better educated, and never are wrong.

3. Staff members are trustworthy and honest, while offenders are untrustworthy liars.

4. Staff members rarely make mistakes and therefore need

not be held accountable for their actions. Conversely, offenders are screw-ups, always in the wrong, and must be held accountable for their actions.

Unfortunately, offenders behave far too often in the above manners, thus validating this worldview. Offenders are seen monolithically by many staff while many offenders view staff in the same manner. There has to be some basis in fact for such stereotypes to exist, but there are always exceptions to the rule. Both staff and offenders are flawed human beings and should accept each other as such.

The best way to describe staff behavior is to use an economic principle called Pareto's Law, the 80/20 rule, as a guide. Twenty percent of staff at any given institution will determine what type of environment will exist. If they act in an unprofessional manner, abuse their authority, and mistreat others, a very negative environment will exist. Eighty percent of staff essentially agrees with whatever the other twenty percent do. They ignore abuses and cover up for them when any complaints are filed. Therefore, the eighty percent are as culpable as the twenty percent.

In the next pages, I will report on both negative and positive experiences I have had inside prison, with staff and others. I will present examples of staff unprofessionalism and abuses of authority, as well as actions taken by staff persons who went beyond the call of duty, which left a long-lasting and positive impression on me. I ask that you, the reader, do not confuse quantity with quality. There may be more examples of experiences with staff that are negative, but the quality of the positive experiences cited below brought light into my life when I knew nothing but darkness, when I'd been at the edge of despair.

In the mid 1990's at a prison in Virginia, there was a three year run when two captains and one lieutenant harassed and threatened me. They would put me in M-building segregation (the hole) and just make up an institutional infraction, or violation for which they sent me there. Once they put me M-building in the middle of the night. At about 0200 hours they woke me up from a deep sleep, told me I was obstructing count, and locked me up. I stayed there for several months. I forget what the actual charge they wrote was, but hearing officers pretty often automatically found offenders guilty once a staff member writes a charge, even ones based on blatant lies.

At the hearing to determine whether I was to be let out of the "hole," the assistant warden asked me if I had a problem standing for count. The Major (Chief of Security) leaned over and told him that offenders did not have to stand for count in the middle of the night! He should have known that! I had spent several months in the "hole' for a false charge. Another time while being shaken down, a rookie guard grasped my buttocks, so I stepped away from him and told him to "keep your hands off my ass." The lieutenant locked me up, stating that I had threatened the guard by telling him I would kick his ass! I spent several more months in the hole on another false charge. In this particular instance, several other offenders wrote witness statements on my behalf.

At this particular prison a counselor told me I had a mental problem because I wanted to earn my bachelor's degree. He was upset that I had actually earned it, but nothing like those at another prison were when I earned a master's degree. The school principal, a female, tried to block my exams, to prevent my access to them, lied about it, and then attempted to assign blame to my proctor, David Jobe. She was soon removed, and a new, more helpful principal, Mr. Billingsley, was installed. His secretary, Elizabeth Meador, and David Jobe were both more than helpful. However, the guards tried to block my exams even after I gained the administration's approval. My counselor continuously tried to transfer me to a worse prison in order to sabotage my studies.

The person most angered by my earning a master's degree, however, was the assistant warden, (A.W.), later the warden of this same prison. He did all that he could to sabotage my efforts to earn the degree. It angered him to no end that I actually earned it, and that he could not stop me.

At the graduation ceremony, the director, Walter McFarlane, and Assistant Director, Wallace Sterling of the Department of Correctional Education (DCE) were present; other officials were there, as well. The assistant warden tried to block one of my two guests from the graduation ceremony. Dr. Ted Koebel, who is a professor at Virginia Tech, got in easily, but one of my mentors, Mr. James Good, a retired DCE teacher, initially wasn't allowed in because they had misspelled his last name, placing an 'e' at the end of it. The A.W. had not counted on Mr. Good's connections within the Virginia Department of Corrections. After a short phone call he was quickly allowed in for the graduation.

At my next annual review, my security level was dropped, so I had to transfer to another prison, Greensville Correctional Center. The A.W. marked out my requested transfer locations and made sure I was sent to a higher security level prison where he used to work. Upon my arrival, a lieutenant, a female, informed me that the A.W. had called ahead and warned them that I was a troublemaker. Thus began eight years of conflict with staff and their inmate auxiliary police at this particular prison.

This same lieutenant and a counselor attempted to block a deathbed visit with my dying mother in December of 2003. Ms. Jan Gardner-Harris, the licensed clinical social worker at the nursing home, obtained approval from the Department of Corrections Headquarters for the visit which angered them both.

On the positive side, the two guards who took me to see my mother were very considerate. The lead guard, Mr. Faison, was a former Marine, as am I. He went out of his way to be nice to my mother. My mother suffered from dementia, and when she saw me all shackled up, she said, "Paul, are you in trouble again?" She had forgotten that I had already been in prison for twelve years. Mr. Faison, went out of his way to assure Mom that I was O.K. and that he would look out for me. He even took photos for us and allowed me to have all the time I was permitted to be with my mother. Upon our return to the prison, they allowed me some time so I could get my mind together prior to re-entering the prison. They were very kind to me. Upon my arrival, my nemesis, the lieutenant, started harassing me. I kept my cool due to the kindness of those two guards allowing me time to process my last visit with my dying mother.

In March of 2004, this same lieutenant harassed me during a lockdown for a shakedown (cell search). She called my dying mother all sorts of names! I went to the "hole" due to the lieutenant's having spoken about my mother that way. I spent several months in the "hole". Upon my return to the unit, the lieutenant lied to me, saying all of my property was lost. I forced them to find it! Then this lieutenant filed a complaint stating I was a threat to staff. I then filed a civil rights complaint with the Civil Rights Division of the U.S. Justice Department against that particular lieutenant and another lieutenant. This was the most racist prison I had ever been in. Since the staff could not come after me directly, they had their inmate auxiliary police go out on the recreation yards and in the chow hall to spread falsehoods about me. I was threatened by a dozen or more people in my living area alone. Then they got the gangs after me. I was told I would be killed if I went out on the recreation yard. I went out there daily, though, at one point it was just me and all my enemies. Other offenders were scared to come out on the yard. Then my enemies went to the guards and told them they'd better get me off the yard before they killed me! Why would they tell the guards this if they wished to actually kill me? They were cowards. I was threatened and harassed like this for approximately six months.

I finally received a parole denial and just had enough of all this foolishness. On Christmas morning, after breakfast one of the ringleaders gave me a look, and that did it for me. I went over to him and told him it is time we settled things: to go in to a cell and battle it out. He refused to do so, and I attacked him right there. I spent several months in the "hole" for this. I needed this isolation time though, as I was on the verge of a nervous breakdown. Due to my mentor's influence, I tried to be peaceful, even in the midst of these severe circumstances. Other than Marine Corps boot camp, it was the hardest thing I've ever done in my life.

God was dealing with me throughout this whole ordeal, however, I had placed too much value on my reputation and that is what others thought and said about me. Those people utterly destroyed my reputation via a concerted effort to spread falsehoods about me. I needed to learn that reputation is nothing, but character is what truly matters. A person's character, whoever he or she actually is in private, is of paramount importance. Reputation consists of a person's public persona, whereas character is the person's true, private self.

As a joke, I put in a job application to work in the hole as a maintenance man. The hole had six two floor wings holding a total of 192 cells. The Execution Chamber is attached to the back of Four Wing. I was actually hired, and the paperwork was processed approving the job. On my first day at work the unit manager saw me and said hello. Then he asked if I hadn't just gotten out of the hole. I responded in the affirmative. He told me it was good to see me on the other side of the bars, and I told him it felt better than it looked! This response assured me that he had no issue with me working there.

I had been housed in a cell with one of their auxiliary inmate police, who was tight with one of the assistant wardens. A few weeks after I was hired, I came back to the pod for noon count. My celly was on his bed watching television. We even spoke a few minutes. Another guy I knew came by to ask me a question. I answered him, and he went on his way. My celly jumped up, telling me he would not stand for people coming to the cell and talking while he was sleeping! I told him that he must have lost his mind, for he was not sleeping in the first place and that he does not control who I talk to or when. Also, if he did not like it, we can close the cell door and settle it like men. He immediately backtracked, apologized, and sat down on his bunk.

The next day at noon count I am told to pack my property, for I'm being moved to another unit. (This prison has three units, essentially three prisons within one location.) I tell my coworker to tell my boss about this and that he will have to come and get me the next day to work, for I will not be on the pass list.

The following day my boss comes and escorts me to work. About 10 A.M. he gets a call from the assistant warden, telling him my job is terminated and to escort me off the job and back to my living area. So this auxiliary inmate police had me moved to another unit then fired from my job. Policy stated one must be six months infraction-free in order to get and keep most jobs. Afterward I had security staff and counselors coming to me, asking how I got the job. A counselor had to approve it, and his boss had to sign off, as well. The counselors there as in most places, were lazy and incompetent. This one hadn't even checked to see when my last charge had been.

You would think this all would be a bad thing, but it turned out to be a very positive one for me. You see, the heads of both the major gangs lived in my new unit, and I was able to speak with them. I knew one of them from years past, and the other had become a close friend more recently. I explained to both of them how they had been used against me in my former unit by the staff and their auxiliary inmate police. My old friend trusted and believed me immediately. The other did, as well, since my old friend trusted me. However, I told them both to investigate it on their own, to not just take my word on things. They did so and were very angry how their people had been tricked by staff and their minions.

One by one, the people involved were moved to the unit where I now lived. When I caught each one by themselves, without co-conspirators present, all shared the same reaction to my presence: fear. They each looked like 'a deer in the headlights.' Then the cowards once again tried to start in on me, again by spreading falsehoods. I did not even know it until the gang leaders told me. They had informed their members that these folks were working for the police. They also told me that they had warned those involved that if they spoke of me ever again, they would suffer the consequences!

Months later I had an incident with another lieutenant, a sergeant, and several guards. The lieutenant was threatening me, and they all had me cornered outside the pod entrance doors. I told the lieutenant they could beat me down, but I'm going to take him down hard, so to try his hand. Recognizing that I was deadly serious, he instructed me to return to my living area. I did so untouched and unharmed. What I did not know at the time is that the gangs in both pods were watching. They later told me that if I had been touched, those who participated in the beating would have suffered the consequences of their actions. How ironic that the very people the police and their minions tried to trick into harming me were now my loyal defenders!

On a positive note, there were many staff members who did not like what was being done to me. I've even heard them call the inmate auxiliary police cowards. Another positive was that I was able to convince the gang leaders that all guards were not the enemy. I did this by asking them to observe certain staff like Ms. Townes and Ms. Epps, and watch how they behaved toward offenders day in and day out.

I continued to seek to motivate many inmates to continue their education. One gang leader shocked me with his response to my having lobbied for him to take college classes. I showed him some literature on certain college programs and explained that he had business skills but would make more money legitimately on the street if he earned a business degree and applied those skills in his own company. His response floored me. He told me to tell him what to do, and he would do it! I began to explain why he should do this, but he stopped me and told me he trusts me, to just tell him what to do. He enrolled in a degree program, and I helped him a little on his first course, Introduction to Business. Afterward he needed no help. I am very proud of him!

Both gang leaders in the institution agreed to order their members to seek approval from their respective leaders prior to acting on any conflicts. In exchange, the two leaders would try to resolve any conflicts between the two gangs peacefully. That is, until the administration got the bright idea of locking them all up under investigation and transferring them. Next, all hell broke loose with different sets battling for power. The leaders' absence created a power vacuum that was filled by younger, less mature, and more emotional gang members who would naturally resort to violence as a first course of action. Management staff created this situation, which shows how inept they can be.

Another issue that seems to negatively impact offenders, often disproportionately so, is when authorities send undercover agents into the prison system to uncover illegal acts of staff and offenders, alike. They have come in posing as guards and as offenders. However, the prevalent pattern has shown that almost all of the times offenders are indicted and charged, the staff who are guilty usually quietly transferred or discharged. The amazing thing is that most offenders don't believe that this happens, even when forewarned.

For example, a new offender is transferred to an old prison to a pretty wild cellblock. He quickly makes friends, for he is personable. However, one individual just felt something wasn't right about this guy. He warned his friends, but they discounted his warnings. About three months or so later, the new offender is transferred off of the compound.

The guy who warned the others gets locked up in the middle of the night. He happens to see a guy in a suit, carrying a briefcase down the hallway. The guy he sees is the 'new offender' he had a bad feeling about before. A few weeks later, drug indictments are brought up against those who had associated with this undercover officer. None of the guilty staff members are indicted!

Another example of this is an incident when my work supervisor and one of my coworkers tried to set me up with drugs. My old friend whom I had done time with in another prison helped me get a maintenance job on the crew he worked on. Yet another old friend had a cousin who worked on the crew, as well. All was fine until the guy who got me the job was transferred. The cousin and my boss strived to be able to fire me so that the cousin could get one of his friends hired on the crew in my place. They even tried to set me up several times with unauthorized items, but I intuitively knew what they were doing, as did the head maintenance supervisor for the section.

Then one day we go into a pod, and my supervisor and the cousin go up the stairs to a corner cell. They have a lengthy conversation with the guy in the cell, whispering to one another. I'm on the floor below with the tool cart. They come to the cart, pick out some tools and a pair of plastic gloves, and hand them to me. My boss tells me to go clear the drain pipe from the toilet in the corner cell. I go to do so. As I do, I pull out a package approximately two inches thick, four inches wide, and twelve inches long, which contains marijuana. I knew right then I was being set up. I put the package in the plastic bag I had for any trash from the drain and then buttoned up the drain. The guy in the cell asked me if I had found anything. I told him that I had not. I then took the package in the plastic bag and threw it in a trash can sitting right there in the corner. I walked down the stairs to the toolbox. My boss actually asked me if I had found anything! That question let me know he was in on the set up.

You see, the guy in the cell had been searched the night before and had flushed the package. The CCTV cameras were directly focused on his cell. If I had openly brought that package out or tried to keep it I would have been busted on the spot and given a street charge! I did not let them know I knew what they were up to. I was mad as hell but kept it in check.

A day or so afterward the final straw came. I was at the toolbox while my boss and the 'cousin' were working. The cousin sent one of his friends (not a coworker) to me to get something from the toolbox. Another setup! I told him I would not give him anything, that he should have the 'cousin' come and get it himself. The guy who had been sent for the setup asked what I would do if he reached in and got something out. I told him I was not the police, so it was his decision to make. He did so. Immediately my boss started hollering at me. I told him off and exited the pod so that I would not hurt him. I was enraged!

Later that morning, Ms. Robinson, a counselor who was a guard when I went through the conflict with the lieutenant regarding my deathbed visit with my mother, came to me to talk. She told me I had been fired from my job. My boss lied on the form, and I thought Ms. Robinson also said he wrote a charge on me. I started cursing and raising hell. She quickly told me I did not have a charge and asked if I wanted to fight the dismissal, which I did not.

My pod was going to commissary that morning, and I had my commissary bag in my back pocket. So I walked out to the commissary. The maintenance shop is around the corner from the commissary hallway. As I entered the hallway I saw a sight I had never seen before. There were several guards at the end of the hallway, all focused on me. It appears that they thought I came over there to kick my boss's rear end! I felt like it, but thought to myself, "God will always set things straight with him and others." Call it "karma" or sowing and reaping. I've seen God set things straight before.

That thought helped me not to do something stupid. It allowed me to calm down somewhat. Fortunately I did not flip out as I had before with my nemesis, the lieutenant. Only one staff member, Lt. Mason, knew how to talk me down when I got like that. She truly knew what to do and always had my best interests at heart as did Sgt. R. Schumacher at another prison. They both knew how to talk me down when I became so enraged I could hardly speak. I truly needed help in dealing with this. Part of my problem is memory. Past abuses of authority are seared into my memory. So when a new incident occurs, it is not seen as new to me, but is one more on top of hundreds before it. And I react as if this is incident number 1000! I truly needed help in dealing with this. Mr. Thompson assisted me some, and Dr. Sarah Van Valkenburgh was also trying to help me deal with my PTSD and head injury side effects. Fortunately, I finally received proper mental health treatment from Dr. Schneider, psychologist, and Dr. Patel, psychiatrist at Green Rock Correctional Center and later by Dr. Tauson, psychiatrist at Coffeewood Correctional Center.

In addition to the above mentioned persons, while I was incarcerated at Powhatan Correctional Center I was blessed to come into contact with: Mr. James Good, DCE teacher; Mr. Donald Keck, Psychologist; Mr. Harris, Corrections Officer; and Dr. Robert Floyd and Gray Taylor, VVA # 662 sponsors; and a wonderful prison chaplain, William Dent.

I worked for Mr. Good as a teacher's aide for three years. He is a bearded, tall man who is a Mennonite by faith. I watched him each workday for three years, and I witnessed faith in action. He was always firm but fair. He was always kind. He went out and spent his own money on supplies when the budget was short. His advice was always spot on. One day I came to class very upset over something ignorant that a staff member had done but then caught myself. I told

Mr. Good that I should not be upset, for I should be used to this by now. His response was golden: "Paul, did you ever consider that if you were used to this sort of behavior that there might be something wrong with you?" Mr. Good said this in the early 1990s, and I remember it to this day! Despite the opposition of other staff, he encouraged me to complete my bachelor's degree, went out of his way to assist me in doing so, and even proctored my exams. He was truly happy for me when I earned my degree.

Mr. Good, a Mennonite, like my Jewish mentor out in society, Dr. Robert White, encouraged me in inquiring about the Catholic faith. Mr. Good connected me with the people who administered the Mennonite Native Ministries, Ruth and Ray Horst, who became my friends but sadly now are deceased. He also connected me with Gerald Schlabach, a theology professor at the University of St. Thomas, a Catholic university. Mr. Schlabach was raised Mennonite but converted to Catholicism. He considers himself a Mennonite-Catholic and founded "Bridgefolk," a non-profit for Catholics and Mennonites. Gerald connected me with Dr. Stanley Hauerwas, a theologian at Duke University. Both of their writings had a very positive impact on me.

I cannot overstate the positive impact Dr. White and Mr. Good have had on my life. Both remain in contact with me. Ruth Horst wrote and encouraged me for years even as she suffered from severe health problems. I am not ashamed to admit that I love them all very much. And the wonderful thing is they've always accepted me as I am, flaws and all.

Donald Keck was a psychologist from Oceanside, California. He would loan me books to read like Victor Frankl's *Man's Search for Meaning*. He tried to assist me in learning how to effectively communicate with staff. I'm sorry to say that I was not a very good student.

Mr. Harris was a correctional officer who had a calm, peaceful demeanor. I don't know what it was, but every time I saw him I just felt compelled to curse him out and often did so. One day, it hit me that I had been such a jerk to him. I sought him out, and I profusely apologized to him. He immediately accepted my apology. I asked him why he didn't take advantage of all the opportunities he had to retaliate against me. I felt it was deserved, but he had not done so.

He told me that he knew I wasn't mad at him, but just mad at the world. He never took my actions personally. His kindness had a very positive impact on me.

I am a former Marine, thus I was allowed to join the Vietnam Veterans of America Incarcerated Chapter # 682 at Powhatan Correctional Center as an associate member. Dr. Robert Floyd and Gray Taylor were our outside sponsors. Dr. Floyd was a Marine who had fought in World War II. After the war, he went to seminary school and became a minister and later became an Army chaplain in Korea, Vietnam, and in the first Gulf War. During the Korean War he rescued a young Korean orphan and paid for his living expenses and education. The boy eventually became the president of the largest Christian university in South Korea.

In Vietnam Dr. Floyd met up with his neighbor's son, Gray Taylor who was in the Army as well. Gray suffered from PTSD for years, and Dr. Floyd assisted him the best he could. Gray developed a successful insurance company after he left the army, but gave it up to earn his Master's in Special Education, becoming a teacher of troubled kids at Thomas Dale High School in Chesterfield County, Virginia. Over time he brought many of his troubled kids to our meetings in the prison so that we could counsel them. Most of these kids went on to do very well in life. Both men had a heart for service and for incarcerated veterans. Sadly Dr. Floyd has gone to be with the Lord.

Chapter 6
Fraud, Waste, and Abuse

SOME OF THE laziest, most corrupt people I've ever met in life I have met in prison. I am sure you are thinking this is no surprise, as I am surrounded by crooks and criminals. However, I am not speaking of those I am incarcerated with, but of those who are employed directly or indirectly by the prison system.

While barely registering with the general public, an inordinate amount of fraud, waste, and abuse of public funds consistently occurs year after year. The mainstream press rarely reports on the cases that actually come to light. While reported cases are voluminous, they are only the tip of the iceberg compared to unreported cases which are exponentially more numerous.

Fortunately, there exists a publication that does report on such cases. "Prison Legal News" has provided the public a great service for many years. Unfortunately, much of the general public has never heard of it. It is my hope that this will change as taxpayers become more aware of how much of their hard-earned money is being misused, misappropriated, and outright stolen.

FRAUD

There are too many cases of fraud that I personally know of to mention them all. I will report on a few so you can receive a very small sample of how corrupt prisons are. Of the instances reported here, the first five occurred at just one prison. Multiply these events over the number of prisons within one state or within the entire country, and you will soon come to understand the enormity of this problem.

One such incident occurred where a high-ranking correctional officer colluded with several of his peers and his wife to receive two paychecks each pay period instead of just the one they earned. His wife worked in the prison business office and cut the checks. Once he was caught, it was all kept quiet. The wife resigned from her job, and all the co-conspirators repaid the overpayment. Not one staff member was charged with the criminal acts they all committed! For several years offender-led groups combined efforts to raise $25,000 to install a cable television system at the prison. One day the $25,000 disappeared from the institution's accounting records. The $25,000 was never recovered, nor was it ever seriously accounted for.

A clerk in the prison business office stole prisoners' incoming money orders over a several month period. She cashed them at a convenience store in Richmond, Virginia. To my knowledge, no criminal charges were ever filed. However, she did resign from her position. From that point onward, all incoming money orders were required to have not only the payee's name, but also his identification number validating the document.

Then there was a crooked prison property officer who colluded with his nephew to require prisoners to send out televisions needing repair to the nephew's shop. The nephew would then 'repair' the televisions so that they would only work for a while and then need repairing once again. Oftentimes prisoners would get fed up and refuse to pay their bills, allowing the nephew to keep their televisions. A prisoner who lived in the area reported that the officer and his nephew would sell the televisions every weekend at a local flea market.

This same property officer stole a prisoner's gold chain and sold it. He did not count on being sued in court over the stolen property. The officer had to pay for what he had stolen, but again no criminal charges were filed. Finally, at this same prison the assistant warden (now a warden at another prison) stole several hundred dollars' worth of food from the prison kitchen to take home for personal use.

I personally know of doctors who consistently take prisoners off their medications without any examination. Many of these doctors cannot even speak English. One doctor would not even look at patients, nor would she physically examine anyone. She only looked at their files, sat facing away from them, and made decisions without even looking at patients; the only time she would actually look at a patient was when he entered the room. It took me nine months of filing complaints to see her.

I needed results from a blood test taken nine months earlier for a skin rash I'd been suffering. She refused to even look at me or examine the rash. Then she tried to tell me why I was there to begin with. I told her I had filed the complaints in order to see her, so I was well aware of why I was there. She then called the guards to terminate my appointment without providing the blood test results or examining my rash. In the grand scheme of things, this was a minor example, but unfortunately the policy of delaying treatment as long possible ends up causing hundreds of deaths each year nationwide.

If possible, prisons deny treatment entirely. "Prison Legal News" has reported on hundreds of these cases over the years. In some cases, staff bonuses are determined by the amount of funds saved each quarter! The savings are clearly the priority, not the offenders' healthcare needs. Prison systems constantly are getting sued for these deaths, but they see it as a minor cost of doing business!

I've seen medical staff delay or deny treatment to numerous persons that resulted in death. This is a massive problem nationwide. Even in prison medical units there is widespread incompetence and deliberate indifference to prisoners' healthcare needs.

Nurse managers often discourage any doctors who act in a professional manner, actually trying to treat patients. One such nurse manager had the nerve to brag about how good their end of life care was for prisoners. She neglected to mention that it is actually due to delayed treatment and denial of care that the need for end of life care often arises!

In one instance, an old fellow's toe actually fell off! Medical personal stated that it was not an emergency and that he would be scheduled to see the doctor in a week or two. Another fellow complained of chest pains, was given heartburn medicine, and later told to return to his living unit. He fell down with a heart attack just outside of the medical unit, on his way back to his cell.

Even when guards do call over the radio about medical emergencies, they are not taken seriously, as I witnessed with one fellow's death during the late 1990s. His mother had recently passed away, and he had been on the basketball court shooting baskets, trying to relieve some stress. He fell out, and the guards almost immediately called it in. Approximately ten to fifteen minutes later two nurses came strolling leisurely along, laughing and joking the whole way. Finally, they reached the guy who by then was dead. Then and only then did they panic. This is typical of what happens when the guards actually do call for help!

There are many instances in which I've witnessed other jail and prison staff alike ignoring cries for help, resulting in the deaths of offenders. Prior to coming to prison in Virginia, I was housed in a county jail. Once in the cellblock I was housed in, an old man fell out. Another prisoner kicked on the steel door to the cellblock for over half an hour to get help. The sound reverberated throughout the entire jail. When the guard finally came, his response was, "Oh, he will be alright," and then he left. When another guard eventually did his rounds, the old man was dead. They had let him die!

At another prison there were several instances of deliberate indifference to offender healthcare needs. I will only cite two examples here. The first involves a friend of mine who had a heart attack on the recreation yard. Other offenders called for the guard who was standing at the recreation yard fence dividing the yard in two parts.

He was talking to another guard on the other side of the fence. He ignored the calls for help and kept talking. The female guard in the tower called for him both verbally and over the radio, but he continued to ignore the situation. To give her due credit, the female guard quickly called medical, and they arrived shortly thereafter. My friend was taken up to the sally port, where an ambulance was awaiting him. However, the guards insisted on handcuffing and shackling him. The paramedics told medical they could not transport him in that situation because they may need to shock him while en route to the hospital. This went on for many a precious moment until a major officer came out and asked what the holdup was. Once it was explained to him, he ordered the guards to let the patient go uncuffed and unshackled. Fortunately, he did not die during the delay.

The second instance involved the guards allowing an old man to die while he and I were in the hole. We had recreation time on a Friday out in the caged areas, and the old man looked well. Later that evening he fell out on the floor, lying there for hours until the other fellows raised so much hell that the guards finally came. However, all they did was pick him up off the floor and laid him on the bed in his cell. Over the weekend when they delivered meals, the old man told them he could not get the meals, for he could not physically get up from the bed. All weekend they did not feed him, and wrote on the feeding chart that he refused his meals. Medical staff was never called for this situation, not that they would have done much for him on a weekend, anyway. By Monday, the old man was unresponsive. All of the sudden, I see several plainclothes officials coming in, all in a jovial mood, laughing and joking. The green "death wagon" pulls up, and I see two guards, also laughing and joking, carry the man out on a stretcher. He is in a body bag. They open up the back door and throw him in the wagon like a sack of potatoes! Not one staff person showed the least amount of respect toward this fellow. It angered me to no end!

Over the course of my incarceration I've worked in several prison industries. There were instances of fraud in each shop. In the print shop I operated a printing press where high-quality watermarked paper was printed, usually as letterheads. Each official order had the client's name, type of paper, type of ink, and amount of the order to be printed. Once completed, it was inspected, wrapped, and shipped out on pallets by the shipping department.

However, on almost a daily basis, I was given "unofficial" orders to print. Most were for businesses that state law forbids prisons to do work for. I would print the orders as commanded. Print shop supervisors would then take the orders from the sally port personally and place them in their private vehicles. None of these orders were ever shipped out with the official ones. On average, the unofficial orders I printed out were valued at over one thousand dollars per week. Over a few years this adds up, especially if you consider that this is only one instance of fraud in just one shop.

Another source of fraud is food service contracting. These food services companies bid to serve meals at a predetermined cost per meal served. They get paid for every meal tray that comes out from the serving line. Obviously, they are contracted to provide meals prepared in a hygienic manner. Sadly, the opposite is usually true: at one prison I was housed at for eight years, the contractor consistently served meals with items that were supposed to be cooked, but actually were served raw. The salads were as if someone just cut fresh grass and placed it on the tray, dirt and all. Supposedly cooked potatoes were served raw with skins on them, loaded up with dirt. Beans and rice were served uncleaned and uncooked.

Now you may say as offenders we deserve this treatment. However, if so, why are you the tax payer paying for better food at a higher price than what is delivered with each meal? The only time food services served an adequate meal was when dignitaries were on the compound. They are not defrauding me, but you, the tax payer!

WASTE

As if the cost of fraud alone were not enough, millions of dollars are wasted each year due to incompetent staff and policies. There are too many instances to report, however, I will mention a few. A vast amount of the budget is wasted on poor maintenance and construction. This is primarily due to maintenance employees who are unskilled. I've seen them throw out an electric door motor worth several hundred dollars because it needed a seventy five cent screw. They never work a full day either, because several hours of the day are spent waiting to move about the prison for counts to clear and so forth. At one location they spent several months to build a pier foundation to set up a doublewide trailer! They even admitted that they did not know what they were doing.

Other examples of waste at first blush may not mean much to you, but if multiplied over many prisons it is a large expenditure. The floors and walls inside prisons are continuously being painted. Oftentimes instead of just cleaning a stain off a wall, they will paint over it. Labor is cheap, for it is contributed by prisoners. It is the cost of the materials themselves that are unnecessary. There are readily available alternatives to spending so much money on these two items.

Prison maintenance employees should be provided with constant training, and protocols should be implemented and enforced to record the effectiveness, efficiency, and quality of the work. However, one glaring item in all areas of prisons is incompetent management. Upper management will issue edicts, but there is no follow through to determine compliance. Procurement policies also limit effective management of funds, and there is entirely too much paperwork within prison systems, much of which is totally unnecessary. One example of this is having to submit reports to order books where the approval is rubber stamped, that is, provisionally approved as long as it complies with the guidelines. This is just one example of when things are done simply to justify a staff position.

COUNSELORS

They do not counsel! They do two things, and many do both poorly. They do paperwork (they call it 'case management'), and they facilitate treatment programs, albeit ineptly. They make offenders take certain treatment programs because they facilitate them. Many programs are essentially worthless as presented; offenders are required to simply check off form items line by line.

An example of such an offender, is a heroin addict, who took no programs for several years and was not required to do so. Shortly before his release, his counselor makes him take a substance abuse class. He tells me he has not thought about heroin in years; now, due to this class, it is all he thinks about. Another offender had a Ph. D. from Columbia University. Since he never graduated from high school, his counselor made him go to school and earn a G.E.D.!

Personally, I've taken two treatment classes that were excellent, both taken in the early 1990s. Many that I took later were a waste of time. Just sit there, check the list, and get the certificate. The counselor justifies her job, and you get the required piece of paper.

RECREATION SUPERVISORS

Recreation Supervisors essentially steal paychecks. I've not seen one adequately do his job since the late 1990s. In fact, one hardly ever sees them. It saves taxpayers' money in medical costs if offenders stay fit, yet some prisons neglect to maintain free weights and weight machines. A simple cost-to-benefit calculation will show the value of fitness over the costs of sedentary lifestyles.

HUMAN RIGHTS ADVOCATES (GRIEVANCE COORDINATORS)

While necessary if they properly do their jobs, they often find ways to deny offenders' complaints, legitimate or not. Their purpose is to provide an avenue by which to lodge complaints without having to resort to courts. But they circumvent the very system they are charged with supporting, thereby forcing offenders to complain to the courts, legislators, and others.

When one is forced to lodge complaints outside of the prison, one must recognize that prison administrators are a vindictive lot. If an offender files a complaint to authorities outside of the prison system, administrators come after them. Their official response to such complaints adheres to a specific formula as follows:

1. Be offended one filed a complaint outside the prison system hierarchy.

2. Seek to discredit the complainant. They will cite institutional infractions, and if there are none, they will harass complainants and search their property, looking for anything they can charge one with.

3. Place blame on complainant. They (officials) are never "wrong," and it is always the offender's fault.

4. Act benevolent. For example, in response to one complaint I was recently told that corrections can only offer me opportunities, I have to take advantage of them. This came from the very same warden who blocked my sitting for a tradesman exam via the board of contractors! So before lodging a complaint outside the prison system one must be prepared for harassment and retaliation by prison officials.

VOCATIONAL INSTRUCTORS

Some consistently rely on offender aides to do all their work. Some act more like guards than teachers. One vocational Heating, Ventilation, and Air Conditioning (HVAC) instructor dogs his students, yet signs off on training they never actually receive because it benefits him best this way. He mentors another vocational (upholstery) instructor who previously worked in prison industry but never taught before. This instructor begins the first day by telling students to read chapter one of the book. Ten minutes later he gives a test on the chapter, disregarding complaints that no one is ready. These two guys exhibit how low a threshold there is in hiring for teaching jobs in Virginia's prisons. They will allow prisoners to exit the class to go to medical, commissary, or almost anything else. However, one cannot leave to attend a religious service. But the prison officials back them up.

If it is not in the textbook, many prison vocational teachers don't know it. Some are hired to teach subjects in which they have no direct experience. Text answers are sold to students so they can pass the class and get the certificate, which is useless if one does not know the subject matter. One student who bought the answers was dumb enough to write them verbatim. At this point, the student will state that…! All this hurts those who truly want to learn and begin a career post-incarceration. Such actions hurt offenders in obtaining employment. If a former offender submits a vocational certificate from a prison school but has no real knowledge of the trade, it makes the certificate worthless in the eyes of employers. The next offender who attempts to use his certificate as a credential will most likely not be hired. Former offenders have enough impediments to obtaining lawful employment as it is; the prison system need not add to this by neglecting their duties to the taxpayer, who pays their salaries.

At one point in time, all trade course students had to sit for an end of course comprehensive examination proctored by a third party. This was a quality control measure that ensured that a student had knowledge enough to receive a certificate of completion. Unfortunately, that is no longer the case.

ABUSE

Over the past two decades of my incarceration, I've witnessed and experienced hundreds of instances in which staff members have abused their positions. The end result in each instance may vary, but all share a common element: That is, staff members know they will not be held accountable for their actions.

The following two instances I witnessed myself. Both involved the same guard. At one prison all cell doors will be opened and closed only by the order of a guard in the control room. There exists an integral lock with key to keep the door from being opened. However, there were no keys, so one is left having to trust staff every time one leaves the pod to not open their cell door for unauthorized persons.

One day while most of the pod was out at lunch, a guard let a guy in the pod, opened a cell door, allowed the guy to steal property from the cell, and opened the pod door to allow him to exit with the stolen goods. The guy who lived in the cell returned, found his property stolen, and went to complain to the building sergeant. The sergeant told him it was none of his concern, for the offender to take care of it himself. He knew who stole his property. The thief lived in the adjacent pod. So the guy went to the pod and beat the daylights out of the thief. They both were sent to the hole, but the guard (who knowingly allowed the thievery to take place) and the sergeant, who was derelict in his duties, were not held accountable for their actions.

This same guard allowed a group of guys from upstairs to come in the pod, opening a guy's cell door to let them all in the cell. He closed the door so they could beat and rob the young fellow in the cell. Once they were finished, the guard reopened the door, let them out of the cell, and closed the door again so that no one would see the victim lying on the floor in a puddle of blood. He then opened the pod door so they could exit the pod and return to their upper floor living area.

Sometimes instances such as these have dire consequences for offenders. Recently, a man was executed for murdering two offenders. The first victim was a mentally ill man who would yell and act out. They both were locked in the cell most of the time. The murderer BEGGED staff to move the guy out of the cell. They refused to do so, so he ended up killing the guy. Staff persons were not held accountable for refusing to do their jobs, which resulted in the death of one of the weakest among us. I knew the mentally ill man from our being housed together at another prison.

So, they transfer this murderer from southeast Virginia to southwest Virginia, far on the other side of the state. While out in the caged recreation area he kills another offender. Prior to this he told authorities he would kill again, but they ignored him. They ALLOWED another person to be murdered! Again there was no personal accountability for their deliberate indifference to the safety of offenders. The law protects them. Even if an employee is charged with a crime, the trial is held in areas where the majority of the people in the community work at the prison, are related to or know people who work at the prison, or do business at the prison. So a jury of their peers will not convict them of a crime against an offender. In one state they beat a man on death row until he died. They were charged and found not guilty of murdering this guy. Other than his family, no one gave a damn.

Recently, at a prison in southwest Virginia, guards allegedly beat a handcuffed offender to death. It is reported that he had extreme dental pain and was attempting to pull his teeth out in order to alleviate the pain. Paramedics came but took the body across the state line to a coroner in West Virginia, who refused to release the body, as there were signs that the victim was restrained at the time he was beaten to death.

If the paramedics had taken him to a local coroner, there is a very high chance that no one would have ever heard about this. Guards at this prison brag that they can do whatever they wish to because there is no one to stop them. They are so far removed from Virginia Department of Corrections (VDOC) headquarters in Richmond that they know they are relatively free to do as they wish without consequences.

As offensive as fraud, waste, and abuse are, what is even more offensive to me is that the guilty parties are sticklers for prisoners following the rules, while they violate the law themselves! They tend to be very hypocritical people and deal harshly with any infractions of prison rules by prisoners. An example of this involves two different counselor's reaction to the same situation. The VDOC started having prisoners complete a risk-assessment questionnaire in 2010. The first page began on page seventy or some such high number. I was asked by my counselor at one prison to fill out the questionnaire. I refused to do so because it was incomplete and thus would produce inaccurate results. She had no issue with my refusal.

A short while later I read an interview with the Chairman and

Vice Chair of the Virginia Parole Board in which they stated that they would not use this questionnaire as a risk assessment tool, for it was inaccurate. In 2011, I was transferred to a lower security prison. When my new counselor conducted my annual review, I again refused to fill out the questionnaire. Up until then there was never an issue with my refusal to do so.

Over the next few months I witnessed this counselor show disrespect to almost every prisoner she came into contact with. She refused to do her job, for which she was being paid, and meanwhile her supervisors adamantly refused to deal with her non-compliance. They in fact defended her for refusing to do her job. She consistently refused to see prisoners on her caseload. She rarely showed up in her office, and when she did, she did absolutely nothing. She apparently had the blessing of the warden and other managers to refuse to do her job. There were never any consequences for her actions. After experiencing her nasty demeanor and being talked down to, I refused to see her the next time she did call for me. Evidently this angered her.

On a day she had taken off from work she asked another unsuspecting counselor to call me to see her. I refused to do so. Then a sergeant came, and they wanted to put me in the hole because I did not want to talk to those other people. Finally, the lady asked me to sign a form stating that I was refusing to fill out the questionnaire and understood the consequences of my actions. My counselor had told me earlier that I would lose ninety days of "good time" if I did not fill it out; I would also receive an infraction (for not doing so). So I signed the form.

I had asked for a comprehensive psychological examination in lieu of this inaccurate questionnaire. My request was denied. The next action taken by my counselor shows how freely they can abuse their positions. She did not write a charge or infraction, but dropped my good time earning level from 30 days good time for every 30 days served (30/30) to zero days good time for every 30 days served (0/30).

Due to the loss of good time, my prison sentence was lengthened by 27 months. I filed complaints on this to no avail, for management at the prison and at the regional director's office backed her up. You may think I deserved what I got, and I'll concede—you may be right. However, what is the cost of this action for the taxpayer? The taxpayer will effectively pay (approximately) an additional $54,000 for my initial refusal to complete the questionnaire. The equation is as follows: Questionnaire times the approximate cost of two years additional incarceration equals $54,000.

Nearly a year later I was able to sit for a comprehensive psychological examination and was advised by the psychologist that it was OK for me to fill out the questionnaire, which I did. I accept the consequences of my actions, whether I feel they are just or not. However, I fail to see the logic of the state spending $54, 000 simply because I initially refused to fill out a questionnaire. How does this act benefit the state or its citizens? Why the bait and switch as to what would be the consequences for my refusal? How can state employees refuse to do their jobs and instead of being held accountable, be protected by the warden and management. Why are they allowed to abuse their authority at will? Why the double standard, where only prisoners are held accountable for their actions?

CONCLUSION

Only a few cases of fraud, waste, and abuse are mentioned here. However, the archives of "Prison Legal News" contain years of such reported cases. Taken individually, these cases may not appear to amount to much. However, if each case is multiplied by all the jails, detention centers, juvenile facilities, and prisons in the nation, it soon adds up to a sizeable sum. This is a massive problem that those in authority consistently turn a blind eye toward. As one former prisoner once said, the fences are to keep the general public out, not to keep the offenders in!

The greatest fear of prison management and staff is exposure. They fear that their ineptness and corruption will be exposed to the general public. They especially fear having the manner in which they lie, cheat, and steal, not to mention mistreatment of those under their authority, being laid out for the world to see. The sum of all their fears is that taxpayers will no longer believe the propaganda, the delusion that is being sold to them by their government, that the public will become aware and offended enough to force the system to become open and transparent. Then their money train will come to a screeching halt!

If a light is ever shed on the black hole where tax dollars disappear into, the public may eventually realize how broken America's criminal justice system is. Politicians and those in power deflect your attention from reality by pitting people against each other, either ideologically or in actuality. Do not be fooled, for the only true debate inside federal, state, and local government is how they will spend your money. Not if they spend it, but how.

Due to political patronage, layer after layer of unnecessary positions are added to government payrolls, oftentimes filled by those least qualified to fill such positions. Prisons are examples of staff and managerial positions in which the "Peter Principle," formulated by Peter Lynch, is in full effect. What are needed are not more positions but more competent personnel in the required positions. Daily I witness staff persons who in effect do nothing and get upset if one complains enough to actually force them to perform their duties.

If you asked these people what their function is, they would be hard pressed to give you a sensible answer. I hear them openly advocate limited, smaller government, yet they continue to feed at the trough of the public sector. Many are career government employees. Those who work in the criminal justice system should be held to a higher standard than are offenders, at the very least. Yet the opposite appears to hold true! Contrary to popular opinion, ignorance is not bliss, for it is costly and affords no defense for those who've abdicated their responsibilities as citizens of the republic.

The citizens of this country and of the Commonwealth of Virginia continue to allow this to be the reality. Maybe they prefer the propaganda, the delusion, spoon-fed to them by both major political parties and their minions, for it is troubling, indeed, to accept and live with reality. However, one cannot correct a problem until it is first recognized and addressed. It is my utmost desire that they will begin to recognize the problem and demand change. A good start would be to demand that former U.S. Senator Jim Webb's bill, S.306: "The National Criminal Justice System Act" be enacted. It calls for a blue ribbon and bi-partisan commission of experts to undertake an 18 month top to bottom review of the criminal justice system and offer concrete recommendations for reform. (For updates on the bill, see curenational.org).

Chapter 7
Self-Help and Treatment Programs

THE PROGRAMS THAT exist within the Virginia Department of Corrections (VADOC) today are but a mere shadow of the programs available in years past. That being said, I attempted to obtain information on current programs, including the newly formed re-entry program for this work.

Even though all this information is readily available to the public at large, VADOC refused to allow me to possess any of this information. I find it more than a little puzzling as to why they would deny me this information.

Offenders and staff alike live and work in an environment where trust is essentially nonexistent and paranoia reigns supreme. This is particularly relevant where it concerns programs as most offenders feel suspicious about the true necessity of staff-led programs. We see what's in it for them but not what's in it for us. Conversely, there is less suspicion and more of a buy-in for offender-led programs without staff interference.

In years past there have been numerous offender-led programs. Such programs had a high positive impact on participants, the institution, and the local community. These programs also had charitable projects locally, nationally, and internationally.

"The Creative Workshop" operated the prison newspaper, "The Southside News," whose offender staff interviewed the likes of Joe Gibbs, former Washington Redskins coach, and Chuck Colson, former aide to President Nixon and founder of Prison Fellowship, a nonprofit that brings religious programs and other services to prisoners. Members also completed projects for Mothers Against Drunk Driving (MADD) and provided school supplies for poor elementary school children in Powhatan County where the prison was located.

The Jaycees had several programs, one of which was a homework program that allowed prisoners whose children lived nearby to come to the prison one evening a week so their fathers could spend time with them being fathers, helping them with their homework.

The Muslim community had fundraising projects where they made and sold bean pies, which were very tasty, in order to fund their charitable service projects.

The Vietnam Veterans of America (VVA) Incarcerated Chapter # 682 successfully held fundraising projects, the proceeds from which went to building schools in Vietnam, to erecting the Women's Vietnam Veterans' Memorial in Arlington, Virginia, and to other service projects. It also contributed to PTSD therapy, which I sorely needed. I am not a Vietnam veteran, but I was allowed to join as an associate member, as I am a former Marine.

These types of groups existed throughout the VADOC. They were very beneficial for all concerned; offenders could actively work to make amends to the society whose laws and norms they violated. Each institution experienced fewer behavioral problems due to these programs. The local communities also benefited due to the programs and associated service projects.

At one time, there existed recreational programs that allowed offenders contact with persons outside the prison walls. There were officially sanctioned "power lifting" meets with outside officials and participants coming into the prison for such events. These events were reported in the power lifting magazines. There were traveling prison softball teams who would play one another. Additionally, outside teams, some of whom were even semi-professional, came inside our prison to play our home team.

There were other offender-led programs. These had positive, beneficial effects on both participants and local communities via service projects. Over time, offenders who participated in these programs gained very positive reputations in outside society, which ultimately led to their downfall and almost total demise.

When Governor George Allen entered office, in the early 90's, he brought in former VADOC employee Ron Angelone to be the new director. Angelone left as director of the Nevada prison system several weeks ahead of an ACLU lawsuit which alleged physical abuse of prisoners, as well as financial irregularities concerning companies that contracted with Nevada prison system. As he resigned just prior to the lawsuit being filed, he was not named as the lead defendant of the lawsuit, but his successor and the Attorney General of Nevada were.

Almost immediately after Allen and Angelone took office, Angelone began to institute policies similar to those he had implemented in Nevada, and he ordered his subordinates to begin the dismantling of all offender-led programs. Punishment—not rehabilitation—became the order of the day. The only offender-led program to survive—at least to my knowledge—was the Vietnam Veterans of America (VVA) Incarcerated Chapter # 682.

It is not that the powers that be did not try to shut down this program (even at times by nefarious means), but the VVA was a national organization (not a prison organization); its membership included individuals such as Virginia Senator Tom Bennedetti and others.

Those in authority would do well to consider reinstating offender-led programs. They are very beneficial to prisoners and the prison system due to there being fewer behavioral problems among participants, and they also benefit local communities through program service projects.

TREATMENT PROGRAMS

Treatment programs are offered with the intent of assisting offenders with learning how to think, live, and act in a manner that is acceptable to society. However, the quality of facilitation of such programs, over the past two decades has been very poor, at least in my experience. Facilitators are primarily counselors who attend a seminar and are then considered "qualified" to facilitate a specific treatment program.

Other than a few programs in which I participated, most programs were conducted in a checklist fashion wherein the facilitator either read from the program text or had participants do so, then afterward checking off a box for the area covered. Offenders are forced to participate in such programs so that the so-called counselors can justify their positions. Refusing to participate results in a loss of "good time", thus a longer stay in prison. As I wrote this, I received a notice that I had been enrolled in a treatment program for which I did not sign up, as I had just transferred to this prison and hadn't even met my counselor.

Most offenders, while resenting this type of practice, comply just in order to maintain their good time statuses. One can only imagine their respective mindsets as they "participate" in these "programs." There exists no positive incentive for participation in such programs, only the threat of punishment for non-participation.

I've witnessed offenders who never had a drug or alcohol problem being forced to participate in drug abuse programs. I, on the other hand, am an alcoholic. At one point my counselor and her supervisor tried to force me into attending A.A. meetings, and the facilitator of these meetings didn't have a clue concerning the treatment of alcoholism.

I also had to repeat an anger management class because suddenly my file no longer showed that I had completed this class in 1994. I was forced to repeat the class over ten years later (in 2005). All that did was make me angry! Due to staff incompetence, I was forced to retake the class, which was no help to me, at all. Both classes, as facilitated, were a total waste of time.

One counselor tried to force me into a veteran's program. I was ordered to "voluntarily" participate in a then non-existent program or else be punished by being placed in segregation for my refusal to volunteer. I packed up my belongings and told them to go ahead and lock me up. They ended up not doing so. The counselor was trying to use techniques that his mentor had used for his own promotion. (This mentor had threatened people in order to get them to participate in his own program.)

After trying to lock me up in the morning, that afternoon this counselor had the nerve to try to speak to me as if nothing had happened. This is how far from reality some folks are. I filed a complaint with the governor's office, as well as the Veteran's Administration. The counselor in question was seeking funding, but such funding was contingent upon voluntary, not compulsory, offender participation.

VADOC currently operates "re-entry" programs run by counselors and supervisory staff whose only experiences have been in punishment-only regimes. Some run around like martinets, being tyrannical, abusive of their positional authority, all the while constantly demeaning and harassing program participants. Participants, by the way, are forced to participate or else forfeit good time status, thereby extending the length of time they must spend in prison. Staff is expected to operate rehabilitation programs but some do not have the desire, the knowledge, or the experience to do so. However, some staff members are sincere in that their goal is for offenders to go on and lead a normal life, never to return to prison again. In the end, how one is treated depends on which prison one is housed at.

When I was incarcerated in Florida in the early 1980s, the prison psychologist ran all the treatment programs. All programs were professionally facilitated. At the prison in which I spent most of my time there were three counselors for approximately 1,000 offenders. These counselors performed their duties in a professional manner.

Additionally, I took the "Life Skills" re-entry class at this prison. I not only received a Florida Department of Corrections (FDOC) certificate signed by Director Louie Wainwright, but I also received college credit for the class via Lake City Community College in Lake City, Florida. The possibility of earning college credit presented me with a positive incentive to fully participate in the class.

Again, all programs operated by VADOC should be facilitated or instructed by credentialed, licensed, or degreed professionals, either as employees, contractors, or via a hybrid system. Then VADOC can streamline the required paperwork and eliminate any unnecessary "counselor" positions, thereby making themselves more proficient in the delivery of services in a cost-effective manner.

RELIGIOUS PROGRAMS

VADOC allows prisoners access to certain religious programs. The major issue with such programs is that there exists a system-wide bias of prison administrators and staff against religious programming in general, especially non-Protestant programs and non-Christian faith groups.

Non-Christians encounter much discrimination and harassment. Native Americans must PROVE their faith is valid and also show proof of their race. To my knowledge, no other faith group has to both prove to prison administrators their race and be tested on the tenets of their faith. I helped a Native American group to re-establish their worship services at one prison after being dormant for several years. In order to do so, I had to provide a copy of my birth record to give evidence of my race.

After possession of ceremonial items for the years prior to the re-establishment of services, all of a sudden VADOC headquarters ordered that those items be confiscated. They were never returned. A certain guard who checked the pass list for us to go to the meetings would ask if we minded him calling us "Injun" or "Redskin" (both similar to the 'N' word to us). I told him he could speak as he wished and we would think what we wished about him.

Muslims experience some discrimination, but not as much as

other non-Christian groups, for they do not just sit back and take it, but defend their religious rights, oftentimes vociferously.

Catholics are discriminated against and harassed quite frequently. There appears to be a system-wide bias against Catholics by administrators and staff, alike. Property officers will attempt to deny Catholics the right to possess a rosary. One property officer recently asked me if my copy of the "Catechism of the Catholic Church" was my Bible, and he asked if Catholics were anything like Christians! Many prisoners also believe that Catholics are not Christians.

On numerous occasions and at various prisons, security staff has given notice that Catholic services were cancelled when in fact the volunteers and/or priest were in the chapel area waiting for offenders to arrive. They've also delayed allowing offenders out of their housing units so as to delay the services. They've often held volunteers in other parts of the prison hoping they would eventually get frustrated and quit coming into the prison.

There exists another level of discrimination. After Walter McFarlane and Wallace Sterling retired as the director and assistant director of the prison school system, respectively, a new director was appointed. He began to enforce existing policy in such a manner that openly discriminated against offenders who wished to attend religious services.

The policy held that offender-students were allowed only three unexcused class absences per quarter year. One could have as many excused absences as necessary. Excused absences included medical and counselor appointments and being called out of class by security or by one's supervisor. Even leaving class to go to commissary was an excused absence! An unexcused absence meant one did not go to class without a valid reason for not doing so OR for attending a religious service!

This interpretation of existing policy forced offenders to make a choice between practicing one's religion or attending class. I filed a grievance on this issue, but this new interpretation of policy was upheld by the powers that be. So instead of being kicked out of school for practicing my religion once a week for an hour and a half out of thirty hours of scheduled classes, I chose to withdraw from class.

That interpretation of policy is wrong on any level. Yet, along with other actions by VADOC personnel it presents proof positive of a general bias against religious programming. So much for the separation of church and state!

There exists ample evidence of the value of religious programming, including "Kairos," which comes in to prisons on a regular basis to conduct retreats and reunions for those who have completed a retreat. Offenders who are serious about their religious faiths have very low recidivism rates. They are less likely to reoffend and more likely to be successful in post-prison life. They present few behavioral issues while incarcerated.

It defies logic that the prison system would hold such a bias evidenced by the system-wide repeated actions of administrators and staff. This is especially so since religious programming actually creates an environment which makes staff jobs so much easier and is a positive for all concerned.

VADOC desperately needs to professionalize its management positions, as well as other staff positions. In the end only truly qualified people can provide efficient and effective programming. The standard has been where the less competent but connected had the best career prospects. This is an upside-down standard.

Over the years I've overheard staff complain about low salaries and a lack of respect. There exists a direct correlation between a lack of professionalism within VADOC and simultaneously lower pay and lack of respect from society. Such respect is earned, not given simply because of one's career choice. Any lack of leadership and professionalism within VADOC is not conducive to being respected.

The culture of VADOC has been punitive minded for many years. However, I would be remiss if I did not give Harold Clarke, the current director of VADOC, credit for trying to change the culture of his department and in initiating more personnel training. He would do well to study how the Marine Corps indoctrinates its recruits in its culture primarily and teaches combat skills secondarily.

Each company has a particular culture, whether it is by design or by default. Government agencies, as well, have a specific culture. Only top management can bring about a change of culture within VADOC. It would behoove them to study the culture of the Virginia State Troopers, as well. They are widely respected by the citizens of the Commonwealth of Virginia. Troopers are held to a high standard of conduct, are professionally trained, and have excellent leadership.

At the risk of repeating myself, I must emphasize the need for VADOC to professionalize its management and other staff positions. Requiring only the most minimal of standards and rarely holding staff accountable for their actions is not conducive to a culture of professionalism and competency.

I fully realize that it takes time to change VADOC culture and to professionalize its staff. However, it can and should be done. All stakeholders would benefit from such a change for more competent staff and management will result in saving the state and its taxpayers vast sums of money due to less waste of funds and will require fewer personnel for VADOC to operate.

I do not want to end this chapter without stating that I've met some very decent, competent, and professional people working within VADOC. The problems that exist are systemic, not based purely on a few individuals, for the programs are too numerous for these events to be isolated incidents. It is a systemic and cultural issue that can be corrected.

Of all the staff I've encountered over the years, only the chaplains have been excellent in their overall professional conduct. In the two plus decades of my incarceration, I've encountered only two incompetent chaplains. I cannot come anywhere near that number as it pertains to other VADOC staff positions. In my view, chaplains are the unsung heroes of the prison system, for they not only put up with us offenders, but also hostile staff and management, who place so many restrictions upon them. They are a very dedicated group of people.

I personally owe them a debt of gratitude, specifically to Chaplain William Dent at Powhatan Correctional Center in the early 1990s, and later to Chaplain Louis Collins and Chaplain Beighly at Greensville Correctional Center, and lastly to my friend Chaplain

Tommy Armstrong, at Dillwyn Correctional Center and pastor of Cedar Baptist Church, both located in Dillwyn, Virginia.

We are also blessed to have wonderful volunteers and clergy who sacrifice their time and funds to come inside prisons to minister to us in a variety of ways, the most important being the ministry of presence and acceptance. They exemplify Jesus' teaching on the greatest commandments, which are to love God and to love others, including the least among us, as illustrated in Matthew 25. Those wonderful folks consistently and lovingly put their faith into action. I thank God for them all.

Chapter 8
Educational Opportunities

THE PRIMARY EDUCATIONAL programs within VADOC consist of academic offerings, allowing offenders to earn a General Equivalency Diploma (GED) plus a variety of vocational technical training programs.

With few exceptions, tutors working in the academic classes do the bulk of the work. In my experience, the teachers for the most part do not do any actual teaching, but primarily assign students to tutors and assign texts and subjects to study. Academic teachers have quite a bit of paperwork to keep up with.

Vocational instructors present a mixed bag. Some are excellent at their jobs, while others are incompetent, dishonest, or lazy. Some seem confused as whether they are instructors or guards.

One HVAC instructor consistently falsified training forms, stating that his students received training that they did not in fact receive. He ran roughshod over his students, expelling students from his class for the least little things. He reminds me of Lord Acton's saying: "Power corrupts. Absolute power corrupts absolutely."

Then there was the cabinetmaking class where —get this— students are NOT required to build even one cabinet! Not one! Not only did they not build cabinets, but students could purchase the tests that must be taken in order to graduate from the class. One student was so meticulous in copying the answer to one question that he began to answer like this: "The best answer to this question would be one in which the student states...!"

There was formerly a quality control system in place in which the first day of class the student sat for a pre-test (and again prior to graduation), when a post test was proctored by a third party. One had to pass this test in order to graduate. Unfortunately, this has not been the case for many years now. Quality control measures need to be reinstated. Additionally, VADOC needs to ensure that all educational programming be taught only by qualified, credentialed professionals, whether as employees or contractors.

VADOC would do well to work with the Virginia Community College System (VCCS) to have VADOC treatment and vocational/technical training courses evaluated for college credit. This would serve to raise the quality of such programs, requiring the establishment of a quality control system to maintain a standard level of quality and to offer incentives to offenders for participation in and completion of such programs.

Presently there are few collegiate programs available to the incarcerated since Congress barred prisoners from accessing the Pell Grant program. Since then a lack of funding has been an ongoing issue. When this first occurred, State Delegate Marian Van Landingham and many co-sponsors put forth a bill, subsequently enacted into law, which was intended to provide prisoners access to higher education programs. Sadly, it was never funded.

Regarding educational programs, please read the essay by Mr. James Good, and the attached article written about him by Mr. David Richardson, at the end of this chapter. Regarding collegiate programs, please read the article written by Dr. John Cavan, et. al., also attached to the end of this chapter.

OPTIONS

There are many options available for inmates who seek to further their education beyond the basic GED and vocational programs. However, one must educate one's – self in order to explore available options and to recognize the best options for one's current circumstances and future goals. I first learned of the many options available from a book I purchased in the mid-1980's. It was written by Dr. John Bear, an expert on this subject. The book is now titled *Bear's Guide to Earning Degrees by Distance Learning* by John B. Bear, PhD and Mariah P Bear, M.A. and published by Ten Speed Press, P.O. Box 7123, Berkley, CA. 94707 (www.degree.net). (800-841-BOOK).

It is essentially the bible concerning what was once considered non-traditional methods of earning college credits and degrees. Nowadays these methods are more in the mainstream. The following information included in this chapter originates and is quoted from what I learned from Dr. Bear, not to mention the fact that I used the knowledge attained from his book to earn a Regents Bachelor of Arts degree via West Virginia University (Morgantown, WV.) and a Master of Science degree in Construction Management via Heriot–Watt University (Edinburgh, Scotland) while incarcerated. It is my hope you will find this chapter not only interesting but useful as well.

ACCREDITATIONS

In many countries of the world higher education institutions are operated by the government or are given the right to grant degrees by the government. In the United States that is not the case for these institutions are approved (or accredited) by certain accrediting bodies. Valid (approved) accrediting bodies are recognized by either a government agency [U.S. Department of Education, Accrediting Agency Evaluation Branch, Office of Post-Secondary Education, Washington, D.C. 20202 (www.ed.gov) or 202- 401-2000] or a non-governmental entity [Council of Higher Education Accreditation (CHEA), One Dupont Circle, N.W., Suite 510, Washington, D.C. 200202-1136 (www.chea.org) (E-mail: chea@chea.org) 202-955-6126 or Fax: 202-955-6129].

Any college or university in the U.S. that markets its degrees as accredited should be accredited by an accrediting body that is recognized the U.S. Department or Education of Council of Higher Education Accreditation. So what is accreditation and what purpose does it serve? Accreditation means that experts in higher education have conducted an inspection of the school and found it up to "Generally Accepted Accrediting Principles" recognized throughout the world. Its purpose is to protect the consumer who spends a lot of money to earn a valid degree acceptable to employers in one's prospective career field. It also serves to ensure the legitimacy of the school, guaranteeing a standard level of quality.

There are different types of accrediting bodies: regional, national, and professional. Regional accrediting associations accredit schools and colleges in a defined geographical region. For example, West Virginia University is regionally accredited by The Higher Learning Commission of the North Central Association while the University of Virginia and Virginia Tech are accredited by the Commission on Colleges of the Southern Association of Colleges and Schools. This accreditation covers all degree programs of the institution.

National accrediting associations accredit schools and colleges within the U.S. and its territories. The Distance Education and Training Council is one example, while the Accrediting Council for Independent College and Schools (ACICS) is another. They accredit all degree programs of a given institution.

Professional accrediting associations accredit specific degree programs within a college or university. This can be in addition to any other accreditation held by the institution. For example, a college's Engineering or Engineering Technology degree program would be accredited by the Accreditation Board for Engineering and Technology. There are separate accrediting bodies for Architecture, Business, Nursing, and Medicine, and for a variety of other professions. In career fields where licensure is a necessity, graduation from a program that is professionally accredited is a must.

Accreditation by these bodies provides *prima facie* evidence that a given school is legitimate and maintains a standard level of quality. When dealing with for-profit colleges as seen advertised on television one must recognize the difference between licensure and accreditation. Many of these schools are licensed to operate within a given state but are not accredited. In order to check this out, compare any claims of accreditation with the local state college or university. Additionally, compare costs of these school's programs with those of the state schools offering similar programs.

A college that is only licensed to operate in a given state may be a good school and operating legally. Technical schools are a good example of this. As a consumer you should conduct research on the quality and cost of a program. Valid accreditation ensures a level of quality. See [Petersons, {2000 Lemox Drive, Lawrence-ville, NJ 0848 www.petersons.com/about (800) 338-3282} or to plan college education online www.petersons.com/student edge] publishes very good reference titled: (1). Peterson's Twp-Year College Guide; (2). Peterson's Four-Year College Guide; (3). Peterson's UCEA Independent Study Catalog (which lists correspond-ence courses. UCEA stands for University Continuing Education Association.

FINANCIAL AID

The federal government has numerous financial aid programs based on need. There are grants and loans. Grants, like the Pell grant do not have to be repaid. However, the student must maintain a passing grade-point average. Loans like the Guaranteed Student Loan must be repaid. Payments are deferred as long as the student is enrolled at least half-time in school and maintains passing grades. Military veterans have educational funding programs as well which are managed by the Veteran's Administration. The federal govern-ment also funds the Federal Work-Study Programs where students can work part-time on-campus to subsidize one's education.

Each state also has grant and loan programs. Each state has an office where one can access this information. However, the best source of information is the college or university financial aid office. They will guide the student as to his or her options at no cost to the student. Regardless, it all begins with the student filling out the "FAFSA FORM", which is sent out to be evaluated for eligibility for aid programs. Unfortunately, if one is incarcerated there are limited financial aid options depending on location and availability.

COLLEGE CREDIT OPTIONS

CREDIT-BY-EXAM:

This may also be called an end-of-course exam, challenge exam, or some other term. Essentially the student sits for a final exam for a particular course and if a passing grade is achieved, he or she earns credit for that particular course. I completed my bachelor's degree via this method, after submitting a portfolio of prior learning.

Each college has its own policy regarding the availability of these programs. This information should be listed in the college's catalog. In addition to exams provided by individual colleges, there are other entities who provide exams for credit, some of which are:

1.   Advanced Placement Exam: offered by The College Board.

2.   CLEP Exam: offered by The College Entrance Examination Board.

3.   The DANTES Program: offered by The Defense Activity for Non-Traditional Education Support Program. It was created for members and staff of the military services but may now be available to civilians. It was developed by the Educational Testing Service (ETS)

4.   G.R.E. (The Graduate Record Examination): offered by E.T.S. and is required examination for entry into certain graduate degree programs. However, another option is to utilize the exam to access college credits via Excelsior College (Albany, NY) and Thomas Edison State College (Trenton, NJ). They along with Ohio University's Independent Study Program offer their own exam as well.

CORRESPONDENCE COURSES:

These are delivered via a distance education format. Some are strictly paper-based while others include DVDs of lectures. The student is provided with a course syllabus and lessons to complete, plus exams. Many reputable colleges and universities offer correspondence and internet courses, including Ohio University, LSU (Louisiana State University) and Indiana University among others.

NON-COLLEGIATE TRAINING:

This program allows those who've taken training programs to submit their certifications as evidence of college-level learning, in order to access college credits. Many colleges use the ACE Guides to evaluate training for college credits:

1. The National Guide to Educational Credit for Training programs;

2. Guide to the Evaluation of Educational Experiences in the Armed Forces. They are published by The American Council on Education (ACE), One Dupont Circle, Suite 250, Washington D.C. 20036 (www.acenet.edu) Excelsior College has a "Guide to Educational Programs in Non-Collegiate Organizations." In some cases all one has to do is submit certifications in order to be awarded credit.

A perfect example of certifications providing proof of college-level learning involves NCCER, National Center for Construction Education and Research. Enclosed is a proposal originating from NCCER material that was submitted to Walter McFarlane several years ago involving the NCCER curriculum. He was then the director of the Department of Correctional Education and did bring the NCCER Program into the department's correction training programs.

PROPOSAL FOR UTILIZATION OF NCCR CURRICULUM

RATIONALE

The National Center for Construction Education and Research (NCCER) was established as a not-for-profit 501 (c) 3 education foundation more than a decade ago by eleven of the largest construction companies and representatives from leading contractors, manufacturers, and national trade associations, establishing a quality standard for certification industry.

NCCER curriculum was created by industry-based subject-matter experts and educators. It is affiliated with the University of Florida's M.E. Rinker School of Building Construction. There is also a relationship with Clemson University who offers week-long, on-campus NCCER Construction Management Academies.

NCCER partners are among the major players in the construction industry, as well as being the major employers. They advise NCCER on curriculum update needs and even on the creation of new specialty curriculum. All the contractor associations use NCCER curriculum to train their employers. To get an idea of how large these partners are, the Associated General Contractors of America alone has over 33,000 member companies. The AGC alone is quite large, however, if one combines all the contractor association's membership, it results in a huge employer base who value NCCER training.(See: www.nccer.org)

It is widely acknowledged within the construction industry that there exists a severe shortage of skilled crafts persons and management personnel and that this situation will probably only worsen in the next decade due to an aging workforce and few new entrants into construction professions. The industry has already experienced difficulties due to a lack of skilled personnel, resulting in more rework, longer construction schedules, and the inability to enter into more contracts-for more profitable work. The end result of this is wage inflation, higher construction costs, and lower corporate earnings. The industry is desperately trying to address this issue. In today's construction economy a semi-skilled or skilled worker is a valuable commodity.

An offender who possesses NCCER certification credentials has a great advantage in this economic climate. Traditionally, the construction industry has not deemed felony convictions as a barrier to employment and career advancement. Employer's primary concerns are in one's skills first and foremost, then one's work ethic. Regardless of past criminal history, gender, or any other factors that may be used to discriminate in other industries, one's skill-set and performance determines how far one can advance in the construction industry.

The provision of NCCER accredited training to offenders (male, female, and juvenile) affords the access to valuable credentials that are the gold standard with the industry. Possession of such credentials in combination with the severe shortage of skilled employees, the offender-has a great opportunity to be employed in a well-paying position post-incarceration. This in turn helps lower the recidivism rate and benefit the employer, the offender and his or her family, the community, the taxpayer, and the criminal justice system. If a cost-benefit analysis were conducted comparing the costs of training versus the costs associated with recidivism, training would certainly prove its value.

NCCER entered into an agreement with Pima Community College in Tuscon, Arizona to offer college credits for NCCER Training Certification copies with the appropriate fee and the training will be placed on a transcript along with the appropriate credits. Pima Community College has previously evaluated the NCCER training programs for the college credits so that process need not be repeated unless the programs are altered. [This is similar to the agreement Frederick Community College has with the Emergency Management National Training Center for FEMA training programs.]

DCE should adapt the NCCER training curriculum and work with the members of the Virginia Community College System to evaluate all other training programs for college credit. The Virginia Department of Corrections should be encouraged to follow suit regarding its treatment programs.

<u>PORTFOLIO OF PRIOR LEARNING</u>:

This option allows those who've obtained college-level learning via life or work experience to validate such learning. For example if you viewed Ken Burn's Civil War series on PBS, it is possible to earn college credits in history if you can write what you learned from the program that is the equivalent of a class in that subject.

In order to do this one must learn how to develop a portfolio of prior learning. In my view the best way to do this is to enroll in Indiana University's distance-learning class titled: F400 (Education) (1) Development of the Self-Acquired Competency Portfolio. This award-winning course allowed me to earn 103 semester hours of college credit via a portfolio. It not only gives you all the information and processes needed to develop a portfolio but the one (1) semester hour of credit can be transferred to any other college or university as it is accredited.

External/Distance Learning Degrees

There are many of these programs presently; and many are offered online. For those incarcerated the problem is that many offenders are not allowed internet access for any reason, let alone educational programming. VADOC has resisted this for years, even several years after a law was passed that allowed offenders internet access for educational programming.

In my opinion the best external degree program for those in prison is Ohio University's College Program for the Incarcerated (CPI), Athens, Ohio.

However, it is not inexpensive. Other institutions that have no on-campus requirements are: Excelsior College, Albany, New York; Thomas Edison State College, Trenton, New Jersey; Indiana University, Bloomington, Indiana among others.

Many of these programs allow the student to use flexible means to obtain college credits and to in effect design one's own major area of study. I was able to combine a business major, a psychology minor, and construction-related credits in my WVU Regents Bachelor of Arts degree program.

I transferred in residential credits and distance-learning credits.

I included a "Life Skills" class at a local community college in Florida offered at Baker Correctional Institution in Olustee. It was a re-entry class and I also received a certificate of completion signed by Louie Wainwright, FDOC Director. I also transferred in the (1) credit from the Indiana University "Portfolio" class. I submitted my DD214 from the Marine Corps and was awarded physical education credits.

I then submitted my portfolio of prior learning. I was awarded credits for Firearms and Riflery due to my military service record book entries. I was awarded credit for "Light Construction" based on my (journeyman) Carpenters and Joiners of America membership years ago.

The remainder of the portfolio "College Equivalent Credits" were awarded for programs and a job I had while in prison. I was awarded credits for math and English teaching practicum, and substance abuse education program, two apprenticeships (plumbing and electrical), and a motion and time study in the Virginia Tag Shop. I could have applied for more credits but there came a point in time when I just felt I needed to submit the portfolio, which ultimately resulted in my being awarded 103 semester hours.

Back then the WVU charged a flat $200.00 fee for portfolio evaluation regardless of the number of credits awarded. Gregorio Merced Algarin, loaned me the money and sent it directly to WVU for me. He was a fellow Catholic, and veteran. I truly owe him much gratitude for his act of kindness.

I was awarded the WVU Regents Bachelor of Arts degree in August of 1998. I could not have earned this degree if it was not for Dr. Bear's book and the assistance of others. I had written Dr. Alan Jenks so much in 1994 I guess he decided that the best way to stop my letters was to allow me to enroll in the program! He and Dr. Ann Paterson (who would take his position as director of the RBA Degree Program upon his retirement) were very creative in their approach to my enrollment.

In 1994 WVU required a minimum of 15 semester hours of residential (on-campus) credits in order to graduate. Being incarcerated, there was no way I could do this. So the following action was taken: I was allowed by the WV Board of Regents to use credit-by-examination (CBE) credits as residential credits. If it were not for Dr. Jenks and Dr. Paterson at WVU and Mr. Good helping me inside the prison I would never have achieved my goal of earning a college degree.

A few years later I was blessed to be allowed to enroll in Heriot-Watt University's Master of Science in Construction Management Degree Program [Heriot-Watt University, Edinburgh, Scotland. (www.sbe.hw.ac.uk) Dr. Paterson not only funded the tuition but she served as my American advisor/liaison with HWU and prison administrators.

At HWU, Dr. William Wallace was the director of this program. HWU requires that all external exams be taken on a set day at a set time worldwide. When it was time for my first-year examination the school principal sloughed it off. She initially stated it "was not convenient", then tried to blame the person who was to proctor the exams, Mr. David Jobe. The governing body of HWU wanted to drop me from the program because of this principal's refusal to let me sit for the exams when required. Dr. Wallace fought vociferously for my continuation in the program; thankfully I was allowed to continue my studies.

Fortunately that principal was replaced by Mr. Billingsley; who along with his secretary Elizabeth Meador and the librarian who proctored my exams, David Jobe, went out of their way to assist me in earning my degree.

Even the commissary manager, Mr. Kernodle, assisted me. At one point I needed a calculator for a class. He picked out the best two for the purpose required and offered me the option of choosing which he would order for me. They all were very helpful.

Initially the degree required the completion of several modules and a master's thesis. In my second year HWU offered a nonthesis option, to which I immediately transferred. Each module required a research paper. Dr. Marie Puybaraud, one of my professors along with the postgraduate office assistant sent me piles of research materials over the course of my three years of study. One of these research papers was written by Dr. Ted Koebel of Virginia

Tech, leading to my friendship with him. Mr. Daniels of Daniels Construction, Richmond, Virginia assisted me with accessing research materials from Canada for one of my module papers.

As you can see there was a group of very kind, caring people who assisted me in every step of this process. I feel this was a joint-effort and we all earned this degree. I cannot begin to tell you how grateful I am to each and every one of those folks.

You would be surprised at who will come to your aid as long as you are trying to do the right thing. Remember this: (1) There are always options regardless of your circumstances; (2) If I can do this, especially coming from such a poverty-stricken, illiterate background, so can you.

Dr. Bear's book and those Peterson's Guides should be in every library as a reference material. If they are not, ask that they be added to the inventory. Lastly, I strongly encourage all who wish to further their education to purchase a personal copy of Dr. Bear's book and Peterson's UCEA Independent Study Catalog.

Chapter 9
Education Behind Bars
By James Good, M.S.

The Virginia Department of Correctional Education Meets Need with Opportunity

EARLY YEARS IN CORRECTIONAL EDUCATION

A CAREER IN correctional education was not what I anticipated when I responded to a job ad for teachers to staff a newly opened correctional institution for young adult males near Hagerstown, MD. The plan was to provide basic academic and vocation training to incarcerated young males, many of them from the urban Baltimore area.

I had some previous teaching experience but not within a prison or correctional setting. My only relationship to the prison context was academic, based on a paper written for a social work class in college. Thus my exposure to and preparation for such a challenge was quite limited. But based on the knowledge gained in that small bit of research, my previous teaching experience, and a desire to contribute to a perceived need in our society, I accepted the position of academic teacher in the Maryland Correctional Training Center (MCTC) in 1967, and so began my teaching career.

I served two years in that setting before choosing to leave for further schooling. While working on that degree, an MS in criminology and corrections at Virginia Commonwealth University in Richmond, VA, I found part-time employment at the Virginia State Penitentiary—no longer in existence—which led to full-time work, and eventually to a 30 year career in correctional education with the Virginia Department of Correctional Education.

VDCE HISTORY

Correctional Education was still in its infancy, particularly with respect to adult education, as schooling for incarcerated juveniles was given priority in those earlier years. Education for adult inmates, men and women, concentrated on vocational training as academic training was considered unnecessary.

However, the 1960s and 70s saw an increased interest in and need for academic programs. It was in this milieu that I found myself when I began employment in Hagerstown and later in Richmond. Providing a quality educational program within the traditional prison system was a real challenge. The combination of vying for space and time to hold classes, often in older buildings not designed for such activities, and the limited acceptance of such programs on the part of the prison administrators and staff often proved difficult at best in that setting.

In instances where the correctional staff was willing to cooperate with the educational staff to provide facilities, resources, and personnel, educational opportunities benefitted those inmates who chose to participate. School administrators often faced waiting lists of potential students at both the academic and vocational levels. The desire for education and training on the part of prison inmates was obvious and growing.

In the early 1970s educational administrators and staff made a move to professionalize correctional education in Virginia by removing it from Department of Corrections control and forming a separate state agency to regulate and direct educational affairs within the prison system. The agency was first named the Rehabilitative School Authority but later changed to the Department of

Correctional Education. This structure freed the educational program from the limitations of a system neither designed for nor qualified to deliver educational services to prison residents.

My entrance into prison education on a full-time basis in Virginia began in 1971 at the Deep Meadows Correctional Center, outside of Richmond. The need for full-time employment after two years of part-time work, while pursuing a master's degree was the immediate impetus for taking the position. However, I was never attracted to a corporate or public type of position; rather, the positive experience with the two previous teaching assignments, and my desire to find success in a service type occupation led me to accept the challenge of a career in correctional education. This was a career which many people would not find acceptable, and some may even see it as a "ministry" type of job. Though it was technically not such, I found it challenging and satisfying.

Following several years at DMCC, I transferred to an opening at the Virginia State Penitentiary in Richmond, closer to my home. Eventually the aged penitentiary, the original section having been built in the early 1800s, was closed and taken out of service, with its residents being transferred to other state institutions. I took a position at the Powhatan Correctional Center with the DCE School, part of that time in an administrative position and the rest of it in the classroom, retiring at the end of 2000.

EDUCATION BEHIND BARS

The issue of the role and value of an educational program within a prison setting invariably arises when considering the needs of prison inmates. The proper response to this question is the same as it is on the street – an education is a basic necessity for all persons, whether free or incarcerated. I believe it is even more crucial for a disadvantaged population of our society which many prison inmates represent.

An education program provides the most positive influence and opportunity available for many inmates. More than one student told me that the school was "the only sane place in the institution". The interest and efforts of teachers, vocational or academic, in helping students achieve success in their educational efforts was not lost on them. This was especially true for those students who had not experienced success in the public school system.

Utilizing an individualized approach, with material oriented to adult learners, the DCE staff enabled many students to realize their potential in an academic setting. The positive relationships developed with the instructors in tandem with academic success contributed to a heightened self-concept and achievement level. School personnel often experienced as well the satisfaction of bidding farewell and good wishes to students when they completed their prison time, leaving with a parole plan in one hand and a General Education Development (GED) certificate in the other! This was a highlight for both staff and student in the correctional education system.

There were those students, of course, who struggled to achieve without the desired success, especially in the academic arena, and did not qualify for the GED certificate. But some of those found success in a vocational field, and others continued their educational efforts on the street after release.

The struggle faced by some of the students was poignantly expressed by one in a response to a quote or slogan which I often wrote on the chalkboard for their motivation. To this quote, "The person who is good at making excuses is seldom good for anything else", he responded, 'Sometimes all a fellow has are excuses!" But whether they saw themselves as good at making excuses or achieving at a higher level, the effort and relationships developed in our classrooms was an important achievement in itself.

DEGREES OF EDUCATION

Another level of education behind the walls and inside the fences which I enjoyed being a part of was college classes provided by J. Sargeant Reynolds Community College in Richmond. The college program was made possible through federal government money funded by the Pell Grant. In addition to the usual liberal arts types of classes, computer training courses were made available which were somewhat of a novelty at the time and yet a viable offer. Business classes offered with the computer classes made an appealing combination to some students.

Many residents who had received high school diplomas prior to incarceration, or had earned their GED certificates in prison, availed themselves of the opportunity to attend college classes. The Virginia State Penitentiary, because of its proximity to JSRCC in Richmond, hosted the first classes in the early 1970s, and also held the first graduation ceremony for community college degrees awarded in a state prison in Virginia. It was an honor for both the college and DCE personnel to be involved in this cutting edge academic program. Unfortunately, the funding for the college classes expired some years later, and the money has never been restored.

As a conclusion to this essay, I submit an article from the JSR Journal which appeared in the fall of the 1986-87 school year. It was written by a student of JSRCC and a resident of Powhatan Correctional Center, David Richardson. He deals with education at all levels in the institution, not only the college. Much of his description and characterization of those "opportunities for education" remains true today. The increased use of specialized educational programs for the disadvantaged and often unmotivated student, as well as increased use of technology in the classroom has enhanced both the teaching and learning aspects of the prison classroom. Education behind bars is still very necessary given our growing prison population which often represents the "left behind" element of our society even more than children. Perhaps this article or excerpts from it will help to put this issue into perspective.

Chapter 10
Education Opportunities within Maximum Security Complex
By David Alan Richardson, JSR Student

IN OFFICES ACROSS America it's another typical Monday morning. For one man, casually dressed, sporting a well-trimmed beard accented with grey, there is nothing unusual about this particular Monday. He unlocks the doors to the office and greets fellow workers with a quiet good morning.

The setting is by no means unusual for him, but to millions of Americans it would be an alien world, walking into a maximum security prison to begin a normal working day. Jim Good, Acting Assistant Principal at the state's largest prison, Powhatan Correctional Center, is a seasoned veteran of almost nineteen years in correctional education. He began his prison experience in Maryland, where he was employed for two years before moving to Virginia. When he began his work in 1967, prisons were no doubt very different, but teaching and educational administration has been his entire career. This morning someone asks why he is in correctional education; jokingly, he replies, "for the money." Those who work with him know his dedication comes from something deeper.

Questioned about his observations on important changes in the field of education, he is quick to point out a few of significant value. The move from the traditional one-teacher-one-subject approach to the self-contained classroom is one change. A teacher now handles a variety of subject matter centered on an individualized teaching method, rather than teaching the class as a whole.

Another new and innovative approach possible to correctional education is the introduction of computers. Provided appropriate software is available, computers would free the teacher to give more time to students who prefer or need additional help. Mr. Good is quick to point out some students may not respond as well to computers as with person-to-person instruction. While most students may find computers an enjoyable tool for learning, for others the machine may be too impersonal.

Computers also play an important role for the administrator. Their benefits lie in simplifying and expediting the large volume of record keeping necessary in the educational department.

Currently Mr. Good reports a wide range of programs at Powhatan Correctional Center. These include academic studies in the classroom, and a tutoring program that utilizes inmate volunteers. Both of these are aimed at helping students obtain a G.E.D. Certificate. Several vocational type programs are available which involve class work and on the job training. In addition, college courses are available on-site in cooperation with J. Sargeant Reynolds Community College.

Numerous students indicate that correctional education is the most positive experience available to an inmate. Benefits come in the way of relationships with the educational staff, and a furthering of general educational skills and knowledge. Mr. Good points out that often security, work, or other institutional considerations can thwart the efforts of the school and of students' obtaining goals. He feels that recent efforts by Governor Gerald Baliles to connect parole considerations to educational involvement are worthwhile. Still even this is not enough unless cooperation at all levels of the correctional system is accomplished.

The single most important aspect of correctional education is the service it provides to the individual. Assisting students to overcome, in many cases, a failure-oriented background, and to develop a sense of achievement and success through an increased educational level, and possibly a G.E.D. or vocational certificate is the ultimate purpose of correctional education.

When asked about arrogance and violence inside the prison school setting, Mr. Good reported, "Behavioral problems have been only a minor source of trouble in my experience. Students' attitudes and problems have been more related to lack of motivation, initiative, and belief in one's ability to achieve and succeed. Students attend school voluntarily, but constantly struggle to overcome these attitudes and feelings, which for the most part stem from their past."

From his years of experience Mr. Good relates that teaching and working in a correctional setting is an education in itself. As is true in any occupation, there are negative aspects involved, but generally staff in correctional education have found success and satisfaction to a great extent. He feels that there is a distinct reward in working with education in corrections, and there are "no parents or PTA's to deal with!"

On the question of whether the public as a whole is uninformed or misinformed concerning correctional education, Mr. Good is of the opinion that society is generally un-informed. This is true for a combination of reasons. First is the fact that the public, for the most part, is simply unconcerned. Other reasons stem from the fact that little effort has been made to provide information to the public in most cases.

Though this has been a somewhat abbreviated look at correctional education, one subject should be addressed before coming to a close. How can education inside prisons find fuller meaning, continue to prosper, and meet new goals? Mr. Good feels this can be accomplished by the general public, through the state legislature, with the Department of Corrections, and the Department of Correctional Education working hand in hand to provide adequate opportunities for prison population. The most important components to insure

130   Paul L. Martin, M.Sc.

this are adequate funding, competent personnel, and a wide variety of educational programs.

Yes, positive changes have been made for the better, but we have a long way to go. Opportunity in education is a step in the right direction for rehabilitation.

Chapter 11:
Campus Within Walls
By Dr. John Cavan, et. al

CHALLENGE

According to the latest data available from the Virginia Department of Corrections (DOC), about 29 percent of inmates are re-incarcerated within three years of being released from prison. This alone costs Virginians millions of dollars each year. This is also troubling as inmates are not being rehabilitated and are leaving prison poorly equipped to face life within society. The Virginia Performance report states that recidivism is influenced strongly by economic conditions and employment. For inmates, obtaining employment is often complicated by a number of barriers. These obstacles include: the stigma attached to being an ex-offender; being unprepared for the world of work; and the lack of educational attainment, vocational training, and life skills (Virginia Performs, 2010). The Federal Department of Education published a report in 2009 that demonstrates the key role of partnerships between correctional agencies and community colleges in preparing inmates for success in life after prison. The report states, "Since community colleges are committed to open access admission, they are natural partners for prisons needing support in providing correctional education." The report surveyed partnerships between community colleges and prison systems across the country. The study concluded that partnerships between creative community colleges and professional corrections systems benefit the inmate, the college, the correctional agency, and the taxpayer (USDOE, 2009). Other research has found that inmates who are fortunate enough to attain a degree while incarcerated are more than twice as likely to gain employment and be successful once released as those who do not. The answer to the problem seems apparent: Simply remove the barriers that keep inmates from earning their degree. Unfortunately it is not that simple. Often, offenders are transferred to multiple locations during their sentence, making it nearly impossible for them to be part of a cohort. One of the biggest obstacles is funding. Tuition has increased dramatically, making the challenge even greater. The Campus Within Walls program seeks to remove these barriers.

PROCESS

Southside Virginia Community College, in cooperation with the Department of Corrections (DOC) has created a Campus Within Walls college program within two of the local prisons located in the college's service area. The goal of the program is to educate college-ready inmates, giving them better preparation for reentry, thus improving their chances for success upon release. The attainment of college credentials by inmates has been proven to reduce the likelihood of recidivism, which costs the Commonwealth of Virginia millions of dollars annually. Such opportunity also serves as a reward and incentive for the inmates who not only qualify for the program's requirements but also model good behavior.

Southside Virginia Community College has the largest service area in the Commonwealth of Virginia, encompassing ten counties and nearly 4,200 square miles. The college has one of the highest graduation rates in the Virginia Community College System, which demonstrates continued support and dedication to its students. The college has a long history working with the Department of Corrections and Division of Education. Currently, the college offers college courses in more than ten Virginia correctional institutions, some located outside its service area. Its comprehensiveness, aggressiveness, and dedication to its mission statement, "that all citizens should be given an opportunity to acquire an educational foundation that develops and extends their skills and knowledge," makes the college the logical partner within the effort to reduce recidivism and prepare inmates for reentry. Such a partnership falls within the Department of Corrections' guiding principle for strategic planning which states "Develop and implement quality programs and services that provide offenders the opportunity for positive change (DOC 2010).

The Campus Within Walls Program has been in operation for two years, and 153 have graduated with a certificate or degree. This represents the largest graduating cohort within a corrections center in Virginia. An amazing amount of collaboration has made this program truly unique. Inmates participating in the program now reside in a "dorm" with study areas, a computer lab, a LAN connection, and whiteboards for tutors. One of the highlights of the college in the dorm CWW is the concept of imbedded teaching assistants (TAs)—eight offenders who have college degrees and serve as assistants to college teachers during classes and as tutors at night and on weekends in the dorm. Further, TAs conduct workshops in Math and English intermittently. Because of this, a learning community has been fostered and is proving to be very beneficial for the participating men. To make this happen, monthly meetings between the prison wardens, college administrators, and teachers are held. This forum allows for the quick identification and removal of barriers which have plagued inmate education for years.

Funding for tuition has been the greatest challenge. The program has been successful in attaining a federal grant and private donation. An advisory board consisting of leaders within the criminal justice field has been established and is helping to plot the future funding model for the program.

IMPACT

The positive impact of this program is apparent. The participants have been encouraged to stretch themselves further than they thought possible. The student success rate for participants is higher than in any other program in Virginia. The pilot has captured the attention of educational leaders statewide. The program has been featured on National Public Radio and in another video, demonstrating the program has gained a lot of attention and helped to spread the word of this unique venture. The video can be viewed at http://www.southside.edu/news/2011/campus_within_walls.asp. The wardens report that there are fewer discipline problems with inmates in the program, and they are seeing requests from the general population to be considered for acceptance into the program. The largest impact the program will have will be demonstrated once the participants are released and enter the workforce. Reducing recidivism for these men will save the Commonwealth of Virginia hundreds of thousands of dollars over the next ten years.

LESSONS LEARNED

This program can easily be replicated within other states. A wide variety of differences exists between regions of the country in terms of inmate education policy; however, some common ideas should be beneficial to all. First, collaboration is a must. There must be close, constant, and constructive communication between the community college and the department of corrections. The belief in the value of such a program cannot exist only at the top of the organizational charts. Each instructor and each corrections officer must be aware of the program and work toward making it successful. Another valuable lesson learned was the great importance of housing the participants together. This allowed for the concentration of resources and the granting of privileges which would not have been possible otherwise. It is also apparent that meeting with the inmates regularly and encouraging them to do well and to take advantage of what the program has to offer has seemed to instill a sense of pride within the group. Any community college trying to replicate this program should first begin by building a strong relationship with their department of corrections and political representatives. The future of the program looks bright. It is hoped that by receiving the prestigious Bellwether Award, the program will gain even more recognition and help to improve inmate education in Virginia and the United States.

The Campus Within Walls has a strong advisory committee consisting of judges, legislators, former employees of the Department of Corrections, director of the State Council for Higher Education in Virginia, and a member of the Supreme Court of Virginia.

It received Virginia Tech's Excellence in Education Award and received recognition from the Association of Community College Trustees.

Several inmates have been released and have been in sustained employment. Portfolios were prepared for each man to include a resume, list of references, and copies of documents and certificates—all their accomplishments during incarceration. These professionally done portfolios had a major effect on attitudes toward what they had done, and what were good visuals for prospective employers.

GOODWILL PARTNERSHIP

Goodwill Industries International, Inc. is one of the partners in the CWW. Their role is to work with the inmates nearing release (within one year or so) participated in a one day class for 12 weeks in life and work skills taught by Goodwill counselors. Goodwill also tracked those men who were released to ensure their compliance with post release requirements in order to give assistance with successful reintegration into their respective communities.

The President will teach in the Correctional Center, and he will pay the tuition for the students in his class. This is his way of "putting money where his mouth is." This is a small way to turn around lives and in turn save the Commonwealth of Virginia resources from recidivism.

Collaboration of Dr. John Cavan (President of Southside Virginia Community College, (Dr. Paula Gastenveld (Daniel Campus Provost, Southside Virginia Community College), and Dr. Chad Patton (Christanna Campus Dean of Instruction, Southside Virginia Community College)

REFERENCES

U.S. Department of Education, Office of Vocational and Adult Education, Partnerships Between Community Colleges and Prisons: Providing Workforce Education and Training to Reduce Recidivism, Washington, D.C., 2009

The Department of Corrections Strategic Plan, retrieved electronically on July 10, 2010 from:
http://www.vadoc.state.va.us/about/strategic.shtm .

Virginia Performs: Measuring What Matters to Virginia, retrieved electronically on July 10, 2010 from:
http://vaperforms.virginia.gov/indicators/publicsafety/recidivism.php

Chapter 12
The Law of Unintended Consequences

THROUGHOUT OUR LIVES we make decisions that have far-reaching and unintended consequences. The same is true for governments when they establish laws, rules, regulations, policies, and programs.

The following will illustrate an unintended consequence of a policy concerning eligibility requirements for low income housing. Years ago, if a family had an able-bodied husband and father, the only way the family could qualify was if the father did not live with the rest of the family. The reasoning was that the government did not want to create a policy that created a moral hazard, or to create a situation whereby able bodied men would choose government assistance over being gainfully employed and supporting their families. At the time it seemed like a reasonable policy.

This well-intentioned policy effectively took the husbands and fathers out of the home, loosening familial ties. It also demoralized the men who were hard working but lacked the education or vocational skills to earn enough money to support their families. What they truly desired and needed was access to educational and career training programs so that they could obtain employment that provided high enough salaries to support their families, negating the need for government assistance.

In my view this policy was the origin of a slide toward skyrocketing numbers of single parent households in America today. One of the unintended consequences of this policy can be seen inside prison walls. This policy encouraged a culture of dependence and entitlement in younger generations. Kids are having kids but few know how to be parents, for many were not effectively parented as children themselves, and easily fall prey to the negative influences of their environments. Society not only accepts the validity of such negative influences, but it sometimes even embraces such lifestyles.

What truly amazes me is that society seems to be surprised at such negative behaviors, and individuals have even begun to fear their own children. One's own parents often have abdicated responsibility, and others essentially write off their children because of the poverty-ridden communities in which they live. Some have tried to address the issue.

Back in the day, there was a misconception that mostly blacks and a smattering of Latinos were on welfare. Numerically there were actually more poor whites on welfare than other races. So, with the exception of racism, all of these folks experience the effects of economic "classism." The policy had a racial element to it, as well.

This nation's criminal justice system reflects the conflict of biases and prejudices of the more affluent against those living in poverty. Why do I make such a statement? I do not know about you, but I have never met (or heard of) an elected politician who was dirt poor! Not one! The more affluent hold a very different worldview than those who live in poverty and this influences the actions they make, particularly concerning the drafting of legislation and the enacting of governmental policies.

The same argument that was made to exclude able-bodied males from low income housing in the past was used to deny prisoners access to the federal Pell Grant program. The primary difference is that those in power (mostly white folk) did not want "educated convicts," meaning mostly poor black folk earning an education. The racial element exists and persists and presents itself in a variety of ways, such as in the disparity in sentencing for crimes involving powder cocaine (most typically sold by whites to whites) as opposed to sentencing for crimes involving crack cocaine (mostly sold by blacks to blacks, poor whites, and Latinos). This disparity has finally been acknowledged and addressed, but it took many a year to do so.

Barring prisoners from the Pell Grant program was an act of ignorance. In economics, one can use a cost-benefit analysis showing that the costs associated with providing a prisoner the opportunity to earn a two year associate's degree at approximately $10,000 tuition costs are far below the net value in economic and social benefits, monetary and otherwise. For example, on average it costs at least $20,000 to incarcerate a person for 12 months. Double this for 24 months, and the sum is now $40,000. This is just the cost to incarcerate, not considering associated costs in arresting, having a trial for, and any subsequent incidentals in the conviction process for any given individual. Most offenders serve more than two years, so the associated costs would increase, but let's just use the two year period of incarceration, at $40,000, as a baseline.

By keeping an offender out of prison for a two year period, the government would save approximately $30,000 right off the bat. Now, let's look at further savings: A person with an associate's degree, at minimum, will have a much higher earning potential than someone who did not graduate high school or earn a G.E.D. Higher incomes also result in governmental savings, for an educated person can better support his or her family, will have less need for government services, such as welfare or food stamps, and will pay taxes on earned income.

This individual will purchase goods and services in the community. He will be an asset to the community, not a liability or drain of resources. Knowing the value of an education firsthand, one will make sure that one's children will be well educated, and this potentially breaks the cycle of poverty and crime.

Instead of those in power enacting legislation and policies that continue the cycle of crime and poverty, they can choose to enact legislation and policies that will break the cycle, thereby saving the government vast sums of money, as less will be spent in the future budgets for arresting, bringing to trial, and incarcerating people; also less will be spent on government assistance for low income families, and many economic and societal benefits will be brought about.

In years past, those in power have chosen fear mongering and demagoguery over pragmatism, for pragmatism does not win elections. Few have the intestinal fortitude to stand up and make the case that the Emperor wears no clothes, yet Jim Webb and Bob McDonnell are two who have.

The remainder of this chapter will consider restorative justice, and it comes directly from the book titled, "Changing Lenses: A New Focus for Crime and Justice" © 1995 by Howard Zehr and published by Herald Press. Dr. Zehr and Herald Press both graciously granted me permission to quote liberally from this text, which I often do verbatim. Any opinions and/or mistakes in this section are mine alone.

Dr. Zehr is currently a professor emeritus at Eastern Mennonite University in Harrisonburg, Virginia, and he is a recognized expert on restorative justice. In his book he contrasts retributive justice, the system currently in place (in the U.S.) with restorative justice, the system we need. He also covers various viewpoints of the United States Criminal Justice System and the various lenses through which crime and justice are viewed. He also explains that although there have been many efforts over the years to reform the criminal justice system, all reform paths have gone astray, and findings have been used for purposes other than originally envisioned, producing unwanted consequences.

Zehr posits that we hold basic assumptions when we identify something as a crime. This in turn shapes our responses to such an event. These assumptions include:

1. Guilt must be fixed.

2. The guilty must get their "just desserts."

3. Just desserts require the infliction of pain.

4. Justice is measured by the process.

5. Breaking of the law defines an offense. Therefore, crime is essentially lawbreaking. When a law is broken, justice involves establishing guilt so that just desserts can be meted out by inflicting pain through a conflict in which rules and intentions are placed above outcomes.

Zehr further tells us that in criminal law, crime is defined as an offense against the state. The state, not the individual, is defined as the victim. The state and only the state may respond. So, the true victim is essentially left out of the process for the most part.

Crime involves injury to the victim, to interpersonal relationships, to the offender, and to the community. Our current system acts in a manner that makes the idea of *community* abstract and impersonal, for it defines the state as the victim. It views wrongful behavior as a violation of rules and views any relationship between victim and offender as irrelevant. Crimes are in effect viewed much differently from other types of wrongs.

A restorative lens identifies people as the victims, not the state, and it recognizes the centrality of the interpersonal dimension. Offenses are defined as personal harms in interpersonal relationships. Our particular worldview determines our views on justice and how it is best administered.

Dr. Zehr contrasts the two worldviews—retributive v. restorative—in peoples' understandings of crime, accountability, and justice as outlined below.

UNDERSTANDINGS OF CRIME

Retributive Lens	Restorative Lens
Crime defined by violation of rules (i.e. broken rules)	Crime defined by harm to people and relationships (i.e., broken relationships)
Harm defined abstractly	Harm defined concretely

Retributive Lens	Restorative Lens
Crime seen as categorically different from other harms and conflicts	Crime recognized as related to other harms and conflicts
The State is the victim	People and relationships are victims
State and offender seen as primary parties	Victim and offender seen as primary parties
Victim's needs and rights ignored	Victim's needs and rights centralized
Interpersonal dimension irrelevant	Interpersonal dimension central
Conflicted nature of crime obscured	Conflicted nature of crime recognized
Wounds of offender peripheral	Wounds of offender important
Offense defined in technical legal terms	Offense understood in full context: moral, social, economic, political

The Bible presents a vision of how people ought to live together in the right relationship with one another. Behaviors labeled as crimes violate such relationships as do a variety of other harms, including acts of injustice and oppression by the powerful against the powerless. Any injustice must be seen holistically, without artificial lines between the crime and other injustices. There exists a whole continuum of harms and conflicts inflicted by individuals, groups, and governments upon others. They are labeled criminal or civil, but regardless of label, harm is harm. Actions can and do injure others. This is nothing new, for even the Old Testament prophets declared structural injustice as sin, warning us that such injustice breeds more injustice.

Zehr asks: "If crime is injury, then what is justice?" He answers the question by stating that if crime harms people, justice should be a search to make things right between people. The central question is not what the offender deserves, nor what should be done to him or her, but what can be done to make things right.

Accountability is a term we often hear bandied about; however, it usually only concerns offenders being held accountable for their actions, which they should be. It is also reasonable to hold the viewpoint that society must also be held accountable; to victims by helping to identify and meet their needs and to offenders by seeking not only to punish but to also seek avenues by which offenders, as well as victims, can be restored and offenders transformed. True accountability is multidimensional and transformational.

UNDERSTANDINGS OF ACCOUNTABILITY

Retributive Lens	Restorative Lens
Wrongs create guilt	Wrongs create liabilities and obligations
Guilt absolute; is 'either/or'	Degrees of responsibility
Guilt indelible	Guilt removable through repentance and reparation
Debt is abstract	Debt is concrete
Debt paid by taking punishment	Debt paid by making right
"Debt" (in the abstract) owed to society	Debt owed to victim first
Accountability as taking one's medicine	Accountability as taking responsibility
Assumes behavior chosen freely	Recognizes differences between potential and actual realization of human freedom
Free will or social determinism	Recognizes role of social context influencing choices without denying personal responsibility

According to the *retributive* justice worldview:

1. Crime violates the state and its laws;

2. Justice focuses on establishing guilt;

3. So that doses of pain can be measured out;

4. Justice is sought through a conflict between adversaries;

5. In which offenders are pitted against state;

6. Rules and intentions outweigh outcomes. One side wins and the other is the losers.

According to the *restorative* justice worldview

1. Crime violates people and relationships;

2. Justice aims to identify needs and obligations;

3. So that things can be made right;

4. Justice encourages dialogue and mutual agreement;

5. Gives victims and offenders central roles;

6. Is judged by the extent to which responsibilities are assumed, needs are met, and healing of individuals and relationships is encouraged.

Justice that seeks first to meet needs and make right looks quite different from justice that has blame and pain at its core. The following chart attempts to contrast some of the characteristics and implications of the two concepts of justice.

UNDERSTANDINGS OF JUSTICE

Retributive Lens	Restorative Lens
Blame fixing central	Problem-solving central
Focus on past	Focus on future
Needs secondary	Needs primary
Battle model; adversarial	Dialogue normative
Emphasizes differences	Searches for commonalities
Imposition of pain considered normative	Restoration and reparation considered normative
One social injury adds to another	Emphasis on repair of social injuries
Harm by offender balanced by harm to offender	Harm by offender balanced by making right
Focus on offender; victim ignored	Victim's needs central
State and offender are key elements	Victim and offender are key elements
Victims lack information	Information provided to victims
Restitution rare	Restitution normal
Victim's account secondary	Victims given chance to give their account
Victim's suffering ignored	Victim's suffering lamented and acknowledged
Action from state to offender; offender passive	Offender given role in solution
State monopoly on response to wrongdoing	Victim, offender, and community roles recognized
Offender has no responsibility for resolution	Offender has major responsibility in resolution

Retributive Lens	Restorative Lens
Outcomes encourage offender irresponsibility	Responsible behavior encouraged
Rituals of personal denunciation and exclusion	Rituals of lament and reordering
Offender denounced	Harmful act denounced
Offender's ties to community weakened	Offender's integration into community increased
Offender seen in fragments, offense being definitional	Offender viewed holistically
Sense of balance through retribution	Sense of balance through restitution
Balance righted by lowering offender	Balance righted by raising both victim and offender
Justice tested by intent and process	Justice tested by its "fruits"
Justice as right rules	Justice as right relationships
Victim-offender relationship ignored	Victim-offender relationship central
Process alienates	Process aims at reconciliation
Response based on offender's consequences of past behavior	Response based on offender's behavior
Repentance and forgiveness discouraged	Repentance and forgiveness encouraged
Proxy professions are the key actors	Victim and offender central; professional help available
Competitive, individualistic values encouraged	Mutuality and cooperation encouraged
Ignores social, economic, and moral context	Total context relevant of behavior
Assumes win-lose outcomes	Makes possible win win outcomes

As one can see, there is a vast gap between these two opposing worldviews. The American criminal justice system has followed the retributive justice model for decades. The facts prove that claims made by proponents of its effectiveness are spurious at best; do not do what needs to be done, and "work" only in the sense we know how to carry it out.

As the old saying goes, it is pure insanity to do the same thing over and over again yet expect a different result. If we use this present practice as a metric, then surely the retributive justice model utilized by the American criminal justice system has shown itself to be illogical, unjust, and defective.

The application of *criminal law* is what triggers the retributive paradigm, yet criminal law is a relatively new addition to Western Society and operates under assumptions that are in many ways at variance with the rest of life. Conversely, *civil law* defines wrongs in terms of injuries and liabilities, rather than in terms of guilt. Therefore, outcomes focus on settlement and restitution, rather than on punishment, yet it lacks the procedural safeguards enshrined in criminal law.

According to John O. Haley, a specialist in Japanese law, the Japanese criminal justice system focuses more on compensation and correction than on punishment. Where the complex, punitive legal system in Western society discourages confession, the Japanese system appears to make it normative.

The basic aim of the criminal process in Japan is to "correct," as well as punish the offender and to work toward reintegrating the offender back into society. Therefore, an offender's attitude, prospects for rehabilitation and integration into society, and acceptance of authority all play a major role in how justice is administered. This is all occurring after the offender has already confessed, repented, and requested absolution from the victim, and has submitted to the mercy of the authorities.

Having had a 99.5% conviction rate, this Japanese model of justice has something to say for itself. However, America has not developed its own culturally accepted model of justice. The problem is not that Westerners fear any form of leniency within their criminal justice system, thinking it would fail to deter crime. Leniency is not the problem; how it is applied is the issue that needs redress. Harsh punishment, such as the death penalty, does not deter crime, for if it did, there would be no more murder, especially in countries where execution is swift. There are still murders in these countries.

Conversely, the lack of a death penalty does not present a moral hazard; people are just not going around killing people willy-nilly because there is no death penalty. The death penalty exacts revenge after the fact but does not deter nor prevent murders from being committed.

While the Japanese have institutionalized the concepts of repentance and forgiveness, the West has not. It seems strange to me that America, a professed "Christian" nation, neglects or misinterprets the biblical view of justice. Instead, America has institutionalized the retributive form of justice, which experience has repeatedly shown to not work well.

As Gandhi once said, if everyone interpreted the meaning of "an eye for an eye" (Leviticus 24) as the Christians do, the whole world would be blind. It was confusing to him that "Christians," so-called followers of Christ, disregarded His teaching on this matter. It is a law of proportion intended to limit rather than encourage revenge. Even in the Old Testament era, cities of refuge (Deuteronomy 19) were established where those who unintentionally killed another could escape revenge and retribution. Another guidepost established the idea that all should be treated alike, the foreigner or stranger, as well as the native.

Biblical justice, even during the Old Testament period, is not to be found in retribution. Motive is an important element in dispensing justice. God's own response to wrongdoing is normative. God punishes, but is also faithful. Israel repeatedly does wrong, and God becomes angry but does not give up on them. He moves, in other words, through wrath to restoration. God's shalom tempers and limits any retributive justice (Leviticus 26; Deuteronomy 4), for God will not give up and will not destroy the sinner, but will be faithful and compassionate.

Leviticus 19:17–18, as translated by Vern Redekop states the following:

"Do not let your mind be filled with hatred toward your brother or sister. Confront your associate, making a strong case to him or her. Don't let yourself get carried away with a wrong course of action (sin). Do not take vengeance, and don't maintain angry feelings against the people in your community. Love your neighbor as yourself. I am your Lord."

Shalom, true peace in our relationship and in our communities is possible if only…we look out for the welfare of one another, even in their wrongdoing. Christ continues this theme in the New Testament, in his parable of the good Samaritan pointing out that our neighbor is not simply one of our own kind, and in expressing what is the greatest of the commandments—love God—love others!

We are to go from retaliation (limited or unlimited) to unlimited love. How well do our contemporary assumptions about justice mesh with biblical justice? The following chart will show us.

CONCEPTS OF JUSTICE

Contemporary	Biblical
Justice divided into areas, each with different rules	Justice seen as integrated whole
Administration of justice as an inquiry into a search for solutions	Administration of justice as guilt
Justice tested by rules, procedures	Justice defined by outcome, substance
Focus on infliction of pain	Focus on making right
Punishment as an end	Punishment in context of redemption, shalom
Rewards based on just desserts, "deserved"	Justice based on need, undeserved
Justice opposed to mercy	Justice based on mercy and love

Contemporary	Biblical
Justice neutral, claiming to treat all equally	Justice both fair and partial
Justice as maintenance of the status quo	Justice as active, progressive, seeking to transform status quo
Focus on guilt and abstract principles	Focus on harm done
Wrong as a violation of rules	Wrong as violation of people, relationship, shalom
Guilt as unforgivable	Guilt forgivable, though obligation exists
Differentiation between "offenders" and others	Recognition that we are offenders
Individuals solely responsible, but in social and political contexts	Individual responsibility, holistic context unimportant
Action as free choice	Action as choice, but with recognition of the power of evil
Law as prohibition	Law as "wise indicator," teacher, point for discussion
Focus on letter of law	Spirit of law as most important
The state as victim	People, shalom, as victim
Justice serves to divide	Justice aims at bringing together

Our system of justice is, above all, a system for making decisions about guilt. Consequently, it focuses on the past. Biblical justice seeks first to solve problems, to find solutions, to make things right, looking toward the future.

Contemporary justice seeks to make sure that people get what they "deserve." Once guilt is established, it delivers pain as punishment; once delivered as such, the process of justice has ended. It totally separates itself from social justice. Usually, pain is administered by sending the person to prison for a long period of time. Once he or she is arrested, tried, and convicted, no further thought is given to what happens to the offender during his or her incarceration.

The entire prison setting is structured to dehumanize. Prisoners are given numbers, standardized clothing, and little or no personal space. They are denied almost all possibility for personal decisions and power. Indeed, the focus of the entire setting is on obedience: learning to take orders. In this situation, a person has few choices. He or she can learn to obey, to be submissive. This is the response the prison system encourages, yet it is the response least likely to encourage a successful transition into free society.

Many offenders got into trouble because of their inability to be self-governing, to take charge of their own lives in a legitimate way. Prison will further deprive them of that ability. It should not be surprising that those who conform to prison rules best are <u>NOT</u> those who make the most successful transition into the community after prison.

Another option for response when confronted by pressure to conform is to rebel. Many do. In part, such rebellion is an attempt to retain a sense of individuality. In general, those who rebel seem to make the transition to free society better than those who conform (although rebellion may make release on parole more unlikely). There are many exceptions: if the rebellion is too violent or too prolonged, a pattern of rebellion and violence may begin to dominate. Jack Abbott is a prisoner who has spent most of his life fighting conformity in prison. His book, *In the Belly of the Beast*, is an articulate, insightful look at the world of prison. After years of being in prison he was released, only to kill again when he perceived that he had been insulted.

A third option is to become devious, to appear to conform while finding ways to retain areas of personal freedom. This leads to another lesson learned in prison: the lesson that manipulation is normal. That is, after all, how one copes in prison. And it is how prison authorities manage prisoners. How else, after all, can so few authorities manage so many prisoners, given such limited resources? In short: the convict learns to con.

Most are in prison due to their inability to make good choices.

So what will they learn in prison? He or she will learn to be dependent, to have a warped ideal of interpersonal relationships, and possess few coping skills. Prison will not teach nonviolent patterns of behavior, nor will imprisonment serve to protect society; for most offenders will eventually be released back into society. Prison is not a deterrent. If anything, after a couple of decades of incarceration, offenders become institutionalized, the extent which varies from individual to individual, but the effect is no less real.

Some offenders become so accustomed to being in prison that it is the only place they feel at home. Some, a few of whom I've known personally, have committed new crimes after release in order to return to prison. One committed thefts and another took a brick and smashed a jewelry store's plate glass window and waited for the police to arrive.

Imprisonment continues to wound already wounded individuals who are not encouraged or allowed to see the real human costs of what they have done. They are punished, thereby held accountable to this extent, but do not feel responsible for their actions. Yet a lack of responsibility is what got them into trouble in the first place. In fact, they will learn the wrong interpersonal skills, and will lose what coping skills they have. They have no way to face up to what they have done or to make things right.

An offender currently has no way to deal with the guilt his offenses have caused himself.

There exists no place in the process for forgiveness, where he can feel he has made things right. Imagine the effect this has on his self-image. His alternatives are few. He can turn his anger on himself and contemplate suicide. He can turn his anger on others. In any case, he will continue to be defined as an offender, long after he has "paid his debt" by taking his punishment. The hatred and violence bred into him in prison may come to replace any sorrow and grief he may have had.

Like the victim of his crime, he will have no opportunity for closure—for putting this all behind him; the wound will continue to be rubbed raw. His term of imprisonment will only aggravate the issue he is already having trouble with. Then he will be released from prison in worse shape than he was when he entered it. There has to be a better way!

There is a better way to handle these issues. Dr. Zehr gives a list of questions to consider in determining what a better way could look like, as follows:

A RESTORATIVE JUSTICE YARDSTICK

1. Do <u>victims</u> experience justice?

   a. Are there sufficient opportunities for them to tell their truth to relevant listeners?

   b. Are they receiving needed compensation or restitution?

   c. Is the injustice adequately acknowledged?

   d. Are they sufficiently protected against further violation?

   e. Does the outcome adequately reflect the severity of the offense?

   f. Are they receiving adequate information about the event, the offender, and the process?

   g. Do they have a voice in the process?

   h. Is the experience of justice adequately public?

   i. Do they have adequate support from others?

   j. Are their families receiving adequate assistance and support?

   k. Are other needs—material, psychological, spiritual—being addressed?

2. Do <u>offenders</u> experience justice?

   a. Are they encouraged to understand and take responsibility for what they have done?

   b. Are misattributions challenged?

   c. Are they provided encouragement and opportunity to make things right?

   d. Are they given the opportunity to participate in the process?

   e. Is there encouragement toward changed behavior (repentance)?

   f. Is there a mechanism for monitoring or verifying changes?

   g. Are their own needs being addressed?

   h. Are the families receiving support and assistance?

3. Is the victim-offender relationship addressed?

   a. Is there opportunity for a meeting--if appropriate--either direct or therapeutic?

   b. Is there opportunity and encouragement for an exchange of information—about the event, about one another?

   c. Are misattributions being challenged?

4. Are community concerns being taken into account?

   a. Is the process and outcome sufficiently public?

b. Is community protection being addressed?

c. Is there need for some restitution or symbolic action for the community?

d. Is the community represented in some way in the process?

5. Is the future being addressed?

a. Are there provisions for solving the problems that led up to this event?

b. Are there provisions for solving the problems caused by this event?

c. Have future intentions been addressed?

d. Are there provisions for monitoring, verifying, and troubleshooting outcomes?

I strongly encourage you to obtain a copy of the text I've quoted so much from in this chapter, as well as other works by Dr. Zehr. I truly believe that no one, citizen or public official, intended for the criminal justice system to produce the negative results that it has for so many years. Even the best of intentions can produce unintended consequences. I urge everyone to accept the facts as they are, bypass any temptation to place blame, and focus on what can be done in order to make the criminal justice system truly effective.

Chapter 13
Proposal for Offender Repatriation Program

OCTOBER 18, 2006

A PROPOSAL DRAFTED by Paul L. Martin and R.W. Vanderwall of Project 35, under the inspiration of Our Lord, who says it is through Saint Luke that we are "to set at liberty them that are bruised" (Luke 4:19).

OBJECTIVE

The Offender Repatriation Program will provide for the restoration of voting rights to all prisoners released to the community through a structured, merit-based, earned-incentive program of five (5) component parts, administered at the local government level. Program provision will be accomplished by establishing the Offender Repatriation Academy (ORA) as the lead agency in partnership with cooperating non-profit organizations and government agencies. The program will be funded through a combination of sources, including private and non-profit organizations, foundations, corporate sponsors, and any available funding from government entities.

Rationale

Over the past thirty (30) years, prison populations in the United States have skyrocketed by more than a thousand (1,000) percent. As a result, vast swaths of the general public have been left without a meaningful voice in the participatory enterprise of self-government. Present voting rights and restoration laws have a disproportionately negative effect on minorities, the uneducated, and citizens of low economic status.

The United States' seeming lack of concern about the growing population of disenfranchised citizens has gained international interest. In July of 2005, the United Nations Human Rights Committee listed as a "subject of concern" the United States' practice of denying the right to vote to nearly five million (5,000,000) felony offenders who have already completed their sentences. In October of 2005, the Grand Chamber of the European Court of Human Rights implicitly criticized the United States when it ruled against the United Kingdom's practice of banning voting rights to incarcerated citizens—a relic of Edwardian history that was codified by the Forfeiture Act of 1870. In a unanimous opinion, the court bluntly rejected the notion "that imprisonment...involves the forfeiture of rights beyond the right to liberty and especially the assertion that voting is a privilege, not a right."

The United States must join the 21st Century. It is therefore of seminal importance that public policy be altered so that people who have transgressed the law can be offered an opportunity to earn anew the rights of full citizenship.

Carrying the label of "convicted felon," even if rightfully applied, is a heavy burden to shoulder for the remainder of one's life. Presently, the restrictions preventing felons from becoming fully integrated citizens of the communities in which they live give rise to a lifetime stigmatization whereby felons feel as though they are always outsiders. Unfortunately, existing restoration laws do not go far enough in providing a released prisoner with a significant or responsive avenue for formal recognition and acceptance back in to the community. Indeed, recidivism rates attest that many of the returning citizens consider themselves as outsiders within the communities in which they live and work.

Adding to this feeling of alienation is the inordinate period of time offenders are disenfranchised. Current law ensures that the vast majority of former prisoners will never have their voting rights restored. Instead, unless something is done, they will live out their lives as aliens in their own homeland.

For a people who hold as formative principles that "All men are Created Equal" and that people are entitled to certain rights as granted by their creator, namely but not limited to "Life, Liberty, and the Pursuit of Happiness", no sanguine individual should also hold that it is permissible, or constitutional, to deprive another person of suffrage for an unreasonable duration of time.

That a citizen may be deprived of suffrage while he or she is sequestered in a facility of physical confinement may be a reasonable and suitable consequence of felonious conduct. However, it is incumbent upon all good citizens to seek the restoration of their fallen neighbors and fellow citizens.

In order to restore offenders as valued members of the community, it is imperative that they be offered the opportunity to resume their rights as returning citizens. Some may harbor concerns that an automatic right of restoration is undesirable. Opponents of restorative suffrage argue that the offender failed to recognize or appreciate the fullness of his or her civic duty prior to the failure in behavior giving rise to a need for incarceration. In the interest of justice, an offender should be made to appreciate what has been lost due to bad acts resulting from poor judgment. He or she must be made to understand the value of the rights enjoyed beforehand, since rights come with responsibility to the community in which one lives.

However, once lessons are learned, the released felon should not be hampered in a sincere desire to participate fully in the electoral process as a consequence of onerous statutory prohibitions. Even immigrants who come from all over the world are offered the opportunity to become full citizens of our great democracy. And rightly so. Yet, native-born citizens—the Commonwealth's own sons and daughters—are denied the same opportunity based solely on past acts resulting from poor decision making.

Therefore, the intention of ORA is not to automatically restore voting rights to offenders; as their actions resulted in the loss of this sacred right, their actions should also determine its restoration. However, there is currently no meaningful and accessible process whereby all offenders can earn back a right guaranteed to them as a birthright. Such a process should include known, achievable milestones that can be satisfied over a reasonable period of time. The ORA program will provide such a mechanism. It will also engender a sense of civic duty in the limits and minds of released offenders. All who participate in the program will do so voluntarily, demonstrating their commitment, their cognizance of the great loss incurred due to poor behavior, their desire to be fully productive members of society, and their intention to take responsible steps toward meaningful reintegration into the communities in which they live.

PROGRAM STRUCTURE

Enactment of the Offender Repatriation Act- such legislation to be drafted in accordance with the program framework proposed herein—will create the Offender Repatriation Academy (the Academy), which shall be:

1. Incorporated as a not-for-profit corporation registered with the State Corporation Commission;

2. Designated as a 501 (C) (3) educational organization pending Internal Revenue Service approval; and

3. (a) Governed by nine (9) initial Directors who shall be appointed from a cross-section of the Commonwealth by the Governor to six (6) year terms. Such terms shall be staggered into three (3) cycles such that three new Directors are appointed in year two (2), year four (4), and year six (6).

4.   (a) The Academy shall be managed by the Executive Director who will oversee all the activities of the program, monitor the quality of services provided, coordinate program needs and objectives, and consult with the Board of Directors on a schedule it shall set. The Executive Director shall also ensure the integration of program objectives with the State Board of Elections and other agencies of government as appropriate.

b.   The Executive Director shall endeavor to establish a regional office in each judicial district within the Commonwealth. The Executive Director shall also appoint one Regional Director for each judicial district. Each Regional Director shall assist in program implementation and development. The Executive Director may also appoint other At-Large Directors on a rational needs basis in accordance with guidelines established by the Board of Directors.

c.   The Executive Director shall oversee and direct, in conjunction with Regional Directors, efforts to train and certify Repatriation Facilitators (Facilitators) who will administer the program at the local level. The Facilitators will be accountable to the Executive Director concurrently. In the event that a local program requires more than one Facilitator, the Regional Director may, after consultation with and approval by the Executive Director, appoint additional Facilitators.

OFFENDER REPATRIATION ACADEMY

THE ACADEMY

The Academy shall consist of five (5) components, the completion of which shall forthwith restore a graduate's right to vote pending certification and registration. The required components are summarized as follows:

1. To have been released from physical confinement;

2. To have been actively engaged in a community for a period of twenty four (24) months;

3. To have successfully completed a program course entitled, "American Political Process";

4. To have completed a minimum of forty (40) hours of community service; and

5. To have obtained a minimum of three (3) character references from any community of people who are not related to the participant.

Under no circumstances are the stipulated periods of time as required by a single program component to be applied exclusive of, or consecutive to, the stipulated period of time required by any other component.

ACADEMY COMPONENTS

COMPONENT ONE

A graduate of the academy shall have fully and successfully completed all periods of physical confinement as required by a sentencing order from a court of competent jurisdiction. For the purposes of this Act, the term "physical confinement" shall be defined as "actual physical confinement in a structure designed or built for the purpose of housing prisoners or previously adjudicated mental health patients." The term "physical confinement" shall not be defined so as to mean any period of supervised or unsupervised probation, parole, or any other imposition of a criminal sentencing act or order.

COMPONENT TWO

A graduate of the Academy shall have been actively engaged in a community for a period of twenty four (24) months. For purposes of this Act, the term "actively engaged" shall include, but shall not be limited to, one or more of the following activities or a combination thereof: Gainful employment; Self-employment; Apprenticeship; Internship; Full-time collegiate or vocational studies; Part-time collegiate or vocational studies in combination with at least one other activity enumerated herein; Homemaker to an employed spouse; Full-time volunteerism; Part-time volunteerism in combination with at least one other activity enumerated herein; Full-time ministry; Caretaker to one's own children or handicapped family member; or any other activity approved by the Board of Directors.

Additionally, a graduate must have successfully complied with all the terms of post-release probation or parole, to include the completion or verified enrollment in any community diversion or treatment programs required as a condition of probation or parole. Facilitators shall consult with local law enforcement agencies, probation and parole officers, and appropriate officers of the court to ensure a graduate's compliance with such terms before certifying program completion.

A graduate's twenty four (24) months of active engagement shall not necessarily begin upon enrollment in the Academy but may be established retroactively by verification of the Facilitator. Nothing shall prevent the period of twenty four (24) months from starting coterminous with a participant's release from physical confinement.

COMPONENT THREE

A graduate of the Academy shall have completed a course entitled "American Political Process; that curriculum will be evaluated and approved by one or more experts selected by the Boards of Directors, and in consultation with the State Boards of Elections and Education. The course curriculum shall be structured to suit the variegated academic backgrounds of participants in order that literacy will not be a bar to successful completion. Sufficient and effective standards of testing will be tailored to assure meaningful graduation.

"American Political Process" will include comprehensive instruction on civic obligations and social responsibilities.

Only certified Facilitators shall be allowed to teach the course. Facilitators shall be knowledgeable about course content, teaching methods, and other reasonable duties associated with such instruction.

The Executive Director shall consult with the Board of Directors to establish specific qualifications expected of Facilitators. The Executive Director shall be responsible to the Board of Directors in assuring implementation of such qualifications. Certification of Facilitators shall be contingent upon the Executive Director's satisfaction that such qualifications in the fullest manner are reasonably achievable.

In no event shall the certification of any Facilitator be contingent upon considerations of race, sex, ethnicity, religion, political party affiliation, sexual persuasion, or any prior condition of legal status.

Course availability shall be aggressively promoted in as many local communities as possible. Academy participants in communities without course availability shall be allowed to attend classes offered in other localities. Regional directors shall take steps to ensure course availability to all participants in coordination with the Executive Director.

All participants who take "American Political Process" as required by this component will be required to pay a reasonable fee set on a sliding scale according to financial need. A fee structure shall be recommended by the Executive Director for Board approval annually.

COMPONENT FOUR

A graduate of the Academy shall have completed forty (40) hours of community service consisting of, but not limited to, the following activities:

1. Volunteering with non-profit organizations such as the Salvation Army, Habitat for Humanity, or others previously approved by the Board or Executive Director;

2. Volunteering with sectarian or parochial organizations engaged in charitable activities and previously approved by the Board or the Executive Director;

3. Volunteering with government agencies at any level where needs are identified, particularly the preferential needs of local Boards of Elections; or

4. Volunteering in any other capacity that has been previously approved by the Board or the Executive Director.

COMPONENT FIVE

A graduate of the Academy shall submit a minimum of three (3) letters of good character from any (one) community of people. Letters from a participant's family, whether by blood or marriage, while welcomed, shall not count toward the minimum number required. The Executive Director shall adopt a suitable format for letters of good character that will include a meaningful range of personal observation and assessment. Letters of good character shall be verified where it is possible to do so.

COMPLETION AND CERTIFICATION

Upon successful completion of all components set forth herein, a graduate of the Academy shall be presumed eligible to register as a voter. As evidence of a graduate's successful completion, the Facilitator shall notarize two (2) copies of the "Certificate of Completion." The Facilitator shall retain one copy for local records and send the second copy to the Executive Director.

Upon receipt of a graduate's "Certificate of Completion," the Executive Director shall issue forthwith three (3) certified copies of the Writ of Suffrage" to be distributed as follows:

1. One (1) copy to the successful graduate;

2. One (1) copy to the State board of Elections; and

3. One (1) copy retained at the ORA headquarters.

Upon receipt, the graduate may present his or her copy of the "Writ of Suffrage" to the local registrar for registration purposes. Upon presentment of the Writ, the Registrar must and shall register its rightful bearer to vote in the forthcoming election in accordance with statutes criminalizing election fraud.

REPATRIATION CEREMONIES

The Executive Director shall arrange for the graduates of the Academy to participate in Repatriation Ceremonies at least once a year so they may receive formal recognition and be rewarded for their efforts. The Executive Director shall ensure that a minimum of five (5) such ceremonies occur at different locations throughout the state. The Executive Director shall establish ceremonial standards and objectives and objectives in collaboration with the Board of Directors, and members shall encourage the active participation of state and local dignitaries.

Chapter 14
Proposals for Positive Change

AFTER READING TO this point, I am sure that you, the reader, must think I hate all authority figures in general and those employed by the criminal justice system, in particular. I do not hate the people but the many acts whereby employees have been allowed to abuse their positions of authority without any adverse consequences. It is a systemic problem, not an individual one. Individuals can only abuse their authority because their immediate supervisors and upper management allow it to occur—repeatedly!

This leads to the most glaring flaw of VADOC—its lack of leadership and professionalism. System-wide, staff and management are allowed to abuse their authority. As a matter of fact, I recently witnessed the abuse of authority and other staff and management covering it up.

I had a young cell partner who was constantly getting into trouble. I had been working with him, so he actually got to the point where he was six months charge free and thus eligible for a prison job. However, one guard here had been harassing him and making crude comments with underlying homosexual innuendo. When the guard finds out that my celly is eligible for a job, he immediately intensifies his harassment and ends up writing him a charge. He confiscated a rubber band but later had busted another prisoner with unauthorized pornography and placed that on my celly's charge, as well.

The hearing officer covers for the guard because she will not request the security camera footage to prove the guard essentially made up the charge. My celly then writes a complaint to the Unit Manager, who covers for the guard, as well. In fact, the complaint was mailed to the assistant warden but ended up in the Unit Manager's hands. Go figure!

I assume the guard is a homosexual, since he only makes homosexual-type comments to the younger prisoners. Additionally, they are the only ones he harasses. The PREA (Prison Rape Elimination Act) allows a sexually harassed prisoner to call a hotline for assistance. The problem with it as it is administered here and in other prisons where I've been housed is that if a prisoner reports sexual harassment by staff, the administration immediately punishes the victim by placing him in segregation! This serves to invoke fear of this type of harassment, especially by the most vulnerable. So, in effect, PREA may as not yet exist as it pertains to sexual harassment by staff.

The issue of how PREA related issues are handled needs to be re-examined so as not to punish the victim. False claims against staff should not be allowed to harm staff, yet a claim needs to be made without fear of punishment at the outset. Punishment need only be administered for a false claim.

Systemic acts of injustice are incentivized within VADOC, and hundreds of such acts occur year after year. In my opinion, the best solution is a tripartite one: education, training, and the establishment of a quality control management and assurance system whereby professional standards are maintained.

A two-pronged approach should be utilized with incentives for compliance, and swift and sure adverse consequences for non-compliance. VADOC needs to establish quarterly professional conduct and competency reviews. Those who meet or exceed set standards should be duly recognized, and those who fall short should be counseled and given a remediation action plan, along with guidance and assistance in bringing their competency and conduct up to par.

A set time limit should be required for standards to be met, or the employee will face suspension or termination of employment. Those terminated or who quit their positions while in this status should be flagged in order to prevent any future state employment, at least for the next two years.

Any incentives, monetary or otherwise, should be tied to recidivism rates. Here again, education is key. I'm told that the State of North Carolina has recognized the value of educating offenders and employees, and has implemented an education-focused offender reentry program. Participants can learn a trade or earn an associate degree. This will positively affect their recidivism rates. VADOC should consider such an approach.

In order for VADOC to become what it could be, it needs to make some changes.

I propose the following:

1.   Treatment Program Facilitators—(A) Require proper credentials and licensure. Only dedicated positions utilized, barring non-qualified staff from facilitating programs. (B) If it becomes necessary to use non-qualified staff, as VADOC current practice demonstrates, VADOC should provide recorded instructions and lessons by qualified staff. This would go a long way in improving the facilitation of programs, such as "Thinking for a Change."

2.   Counselors—Re-engineer these positions by drastically reducing required paperwork and requiring a computerized offender file system that is password protected, in order to allow staff access to only specific parts of an offender's file. For example, a vocational instructor could access only an offender's vocational education portion of the file to input data such as course completion, etc. She/he could not access any other parts of the file. This would allow housing supervisors, job supervisors, school

principals, medical staff, and others to access parts of an offender's file that are specific to each staff member's purview. VADOC could then hire lower-paid clerks to manage the data. Additionally, in my experience, the VADOC counselors do not counsel. Any needed counseling would be conducted by mental health staff.

3. <u>Grievance Coordinators</u>—Re-engineer the position. Currently (and for some years) all they do is block and delay valid offender claims. This is not their originally stated purpose.

4. <u>Vocational—Technical Instructors</u>—All instructors must complete an accredited teacher training program and be trade certified and licensed.

5. <u>Collegiate Evaluation</u>—Have all treatment and vocational / technical programs evaluated by the Virginia Community College System (VCCS) for collegiate credit, with corresponding quality control and assurance systems established for all programs.

6. <u>Personal Education Plan</u>—(A) All security staff should have a personal education plan established upon hiring to assist with career advancement. Set educational requirements should be established for each management position from sergeant and above to the Director level. (B) All offenders should have a personal educational plan established upon VADOC entry. (C) Purposed courses for offenders and staff below the rank of sergeant are: Survey of Economics; Consumer Math; Personal Finance; Career Options & Planning; Organizational Behavior; Interpersonal Communications; Social Psychology; Social and Restorative Justice; Emotional Awareness (Houses of Healing); State and Local Government; Critical Thinking; Report Writing; Business Writing

7. <u>Benefit Corporations</u>—Legislation should be enacted to establish a legal process whereby a "Benefit Corporation" can be legally created. It is effectively a hybridized profit and non-profit corporation-business format with a triple bottom line of people, planet, and profits.

Such corporations have a percentage of profits dedicated to a social benefit within the areas they operate. Additional legislation would be enacted to allow benefit corporations to contract with state agencies while holding favored contractor status due to social mission. Within VADOC, a benefit corporation could contract to provide all academic and vocational-technical training programs; all treatment programs; all counseling needs; grievance procedure services; all collegiate and training programs for offenders, staff, and management, among other services.

The following is an undated copy of an Associated Press article written on social benefit corporations several years ago:

STATES MOVE TO LET FIRMS PURSUE SOCIAL MISSIONS

BEN COHEN AND Jerry Greenfield wish a bill making its way through the Vermont Legislature had been law decades ago. If they'd been allowed to set up as a benefit corporation, their Ben & Jerry's Homemade, Inc., the Vermont-based super premium ice cream maker, might not have had to sell out to a British-Dutch conglomerate years ago this week.

Benefit corporations are devoted to a triple bottom line of "people, planet, and profits," said Andrea Cohen of Vermont Business for Social Responsibility.

Under legislation now proposed in Vermont and other states, they'd have their status as a benefit corporation—with an annual report on goals like environmental protection and community involvement—written into their charter. That would better enable them to dodge a takeover based purely on finances.

Senator Hinda Miller, a principal sponsor of the Vermont legislation, said a benefit corporation could resist a takeover bid—and protect its social mission—even in the face of a lucrative price-per-share offer.

"It gives the board of directors the ability to say no to someone who is offering a good price for the stock," said Miller, a Democrat representing Chittendon County. "They can say, 'Thanks for the great price, but we're not going to sell because we have obligations beyond the stock.'"

To earn and maintain its status as a benefit corporation, a company would have to file an annual report, available for public review, listing and detailing progress toward goals like lowering carbon emissions, providing healthcare for part-time workers, or giving employees time off for community service.

Benefit corporation bills have been introduced in Maryland and Vermont and are expected to get a hearing next year in Colorado, North Carolina, Pennsylvania, and Washington state, said Jay Coen Gilbert, cofounder of B Lab, a Philadelphia area nonprofit promoting the benefit corporation idea. Similar legislation is expected to be filed in coming weeks in New York.

Maryland's own legislation has cleared both houses of legislature and is awaiting action by the governor. Vermont's has passed the Senate and is expected to win House approval and then be signed by Governor Jim Douglas.

(Associated Press Article—Montpelier, Vermont)

[End Article]

AFTER DR. ANN Paterson sent me this article, I contacted Vermont State Senator Hinda Miller on this issue. Senator Miller graciously posted copies of the legislation as passed into law. It was very informative. To my knowledge, Maryland's governor, Martin O'Malley signed the legislature. The goal is to get a similar law passed in Virginia and West Virginia. It would benefit all stakeholders if benefit corporations were allowed to exist and were given preference in state and federal contracts.

1. <u>Management Qualifications</u>—(A) In order to attain the rank of sergeant, one must possess an associate degree plus experience. (B) To attain the rank of Captain or its equivalent pay grade (Unit Manager) one must possess a bachelor's degree plus experience. The degree must consist of a major in management with a minor in restorative justice.

2. <u>Educational Technology</u>—The use of technology should be expanded in order to offer online degrees, certificates, diplomas, and noncredit programs to staff and offenders. (See Code of Virginia s 22.1-343 # 4 Powers and Duties of Board)

3. <u>Offender Specific Purpose Built Communities</u>—Many long-term offenders have no permanent residence, and VADOC is fearful of releasing them back into society. Legislation needs to be enacted that will allow a social benefit corporation or nonprofit to seek funding for the provision of a transitional housing from long-term incarceration to freedom. Such an entity could serve bordering states as well as VADOC. The location of such a facility (or facilities) would not necessarily be required to exist within the border of the Commonwealth of Virginia, but should at minimum be required to exist in a bordering state.

Such an entity could be adapted from the Purpose Built Community model (noted in the following article) to meet the needs of the long term incarcerated.

A PROJECT WITH BIG AMBITION

WARREN BUFFET LEADS a troop of officials, reporters, and a guy with a boom mike into a new apartment. Five years ago, after the levees failed, this area was 10 feet underwater. Now, on this bitterly cold morning in March, it's a construction zone ringed by chain link fences, and one of the richest men in America wanders around in what will eventually be some family's home. Model furnishings have been placed just so. The place still smells of new.

This is part of the inaugural meeting of the Purpose Built Communities Network, to which civic leaders from around the country have come. And it is an attempt to export "What Works."

"As is the case with my 2007–2008 series of columns by that name, 'What Works', about programs that have shown success saving young people in crisis," one of the most ambitious of them was the East Lake Foundation in Atlanta, founded in 1995 by developer Tom Cousins.

Cousins achieved near miracles—violent crime down 96% and 78% of kids passing the state math test when only 5% could do it before—in what had been one of the worst and most dangerous public housing projects in the country. There were many elements to that success: offering better schools, creating an early learning center, building a YMCA, evicting felons.

But the centerpiece was that in the airy new apartment complex Cousins built to replace the housing project, half the units are held for middle income families, the other half for poor, government subsidized families. The idea being that middle income people would--just in their daily doings--model the habits and behaviors of a successful life. It worked spectacularly.

And Purpose Built Communities is the outgrowth. Founded by Cousins, Buffet, and philanthropist Julia Robertson, it offers expertise, guidance, and partnership to those seeking to replicate East Lake's success in their own blighted communities. Its member network includes projects in Rome, GA; Jackson, MS; Indianapolis, IN; and Memphis, TN. There is no charge for its services.

Vice President Carol Naughton says community leaders in other cities who want to learn more should visit: purposebuiltcommunities.org. Or, she says: "Give me a call. It's that simple. Give me a call at (404) 591-1400, and we'll start the conversation. We can kind of coach you about how to build this initial organization, about who your partners can be, who can bring resources to the community and advocate for the community, and who those resources are 'within' the community, too."

It is not easy, and it is not magic. It takes time, tears, toil, and setback to grow hope in places where it has not grown before. But do it, says Cousins, and "you will see the children who would've been lost in the normal process become stars, become bright."

"There is," says PBC President Chuck Knapp, "a difference between a project and a movement. They want this to be a movement." "Whenever you have something happen like East Lake," says Buffett, "people say, 'That's just because one guy had a passion for it, wouldn't stop and went through a brick wall, made it happen'. But the real test is whether it's replicable. Once you do it beyond where the founders started it, it becomes evident to other communities: If they care enough about getting it done, it will get done. And this," he says, "needs to get done in dozens of communities. Not just one or two, not just five or six."

(By Leonard Pitts, Jr., © 2010 *Miami Herald*)

[End of article]

GRANTED, EVICTING FELONS will not be a component of what I propose since the purpose of the community will be for felons. Long-term offenders need transitional housing in order to be eased back into society. On a much broader scale, such an entity could assist all felons prior to their total release from their respective prison sentences.

4. The National Criminal Justice System Act (S. 306)—was originally sponsored by former US Senator Jim Webb in 2009 and should be enacted. The act would establish a bipartisan commission to study the whole criminal justice system over an 18 month period. A Certified Value Management Professional should act as a consultant to the commission so as to conduct a "charrette," including a "functional analysis" of the whole criminal justice system

and its constituent parts.

5. <u>Offender Repatriation Academy</u>—should be established, inculcating a restorative justice framework in partnership with VADOC.

6. <u>Houses of Healing</u>—is a program developed by Ms. Robin Casarjian, M.A., in Massachusetts. It should be provided system-wide and professionally facilitated as it is at Green Rock Correctional Center in Chatham, Virginia, by Dr. Craig Schneider, psychologist. The program is one of the best I've ever encountered, as is the Father Thomas workshop on "centering prayer," also mentioned in the Houses of Healing text. (See: www.lionheart.org or The Lionheart Foundation, P.O. BOX 170115, Boston, MA 02117)

The enclosed proposals are but a few that I feel will bring about positive change. I am sure there are many other excellent ideas out there. I truly believe that these proposals, if enacted, would benefit all stakeholders—from victims to offenders, staff, and taxpayers. I do not care to place blame for the current ills of the criminal justice system. My overarching concern is that we fix what is so clearly broken. Things can and will improve if only we open our minds to possibilities and tune out the political demagogues whose only goal is to secure their own respective political careers.

Lastly, I sincerely hope that this book is of some help to those who read it in gaining an understanding of the criminal justice system and of prison life. Some funds due to me from the sale of this book will go toward assisting the chaplains of the Virginia prison system. They desperately need any additional funding they can receive. I thank them for their wonderful, selfless work. May God bless and keep them.

A PORTION OF the proceeds from the sales of this book will go to:

GRACEINSIDE

Formerly known as Chaplain Service Prison Ministry of Virginia, Inc.
2828 Emerywood Parkwood
Richmond, Virginia 23294
Phone: 804-358-7650

http://www.graceinside.org

About the Author

PAUL MARTIN HAS a long history of involvement with the criminal justice system. His first contact was with the juvenile system in Virginia. Then, after a stint in the Marine Corps, he served a couple of years in prison in the state of Florida. He spent several years on parole and probation prior to his incarceration in 1991. He was incarcerated in Virginia from 1991 to 2015. Over the years of his incarceration, he learned many valuable lessons which he shares in this work.